Crepe Cookbook

Prepare All Types of Tasty Crepes with an Easy Crepe Cookbook Filled with Delicious Crepe Recipes

By
BookSumo Press

Published by
http://www.booksumo.com

Table of Contents

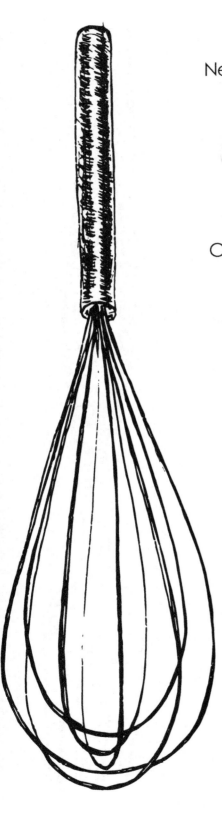

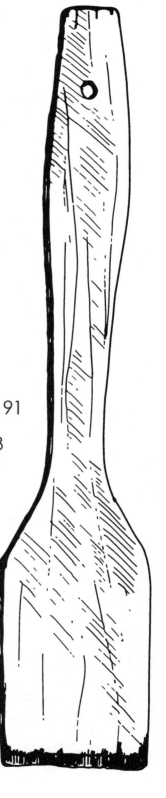

Joe's
Berry Crepes

Prep Time: 30 mins
Total Time: 50 mins

Servings per Recipe: 1
Calories	206.0
Fat	11.5g
Cholesterol	86.6mg
Sodium	195.1mg
Carbohydrates	20.7g
Protein	5.3g

Ingredients

2 C. sliced strawberries
1/4 C. sugar
1 (8 oz.) packages cream cheese
1/4 C. powdered sugar
Crepes
2 tbsp. sugar
1/2 tsp. vanilla

4 eggs
1 1/3 C. milk
2 tbsp. oil
1 C. flour
1/2 tsp. salt

Directions

1. For the strawberry cream: in a bowl, add the sugar and strawberries and toss to coat well. Place in the fridge for all the night.
2. Drain the strawberries completely.
3. In a bowl, add the powdered sugar and cream cheese and beat until smooth. Add the strawberries and gently, stir to combine.
4. For the crepes: in a bowl, add the eggs and beat well.
5. Add the remaining ingredients and mix until well combined.
6. Place in the fridge for up to 2 hours.
7. Place a frying pan over medium-high heat until heated through.
8. Place about 1/8 C. of the mixture and tilt the pan to spread in a thin layer. Cook until golden brown from both sides.
9. Fill each crepe with the strawberry cream evenly.
10. Enjoy.

MAKE AHEAD
Batter

Prep Time: 10 mins

Total Time: 1 hr 30 mins

Servings per Recipe: 1
Calories	54.8
Fat	2.0g
Cholesterol	40.4mg
Sodium	25.4mg
Carbohydrates	6.6g
Protein	2.3g

Ingredients

4 large eggs
1 C. flour
2 tbsp. sugar
1 C. milk

1/4 C. water
1 tbsp. melted butter

Directions

1. In a food processor, add all the ingredients and pulse until smooth.
2. Place in the fridge for about 1 hour.
3. Place a nonstick skillet over medium heat until heated through.
4. Place desired amount of the mixture and tilt the pan to spread in a thin layer.
5. Cook until golden brown from both sides.
6. Remove from the heat and enjoy.

Crepes
for 1

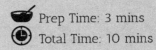 Prep Time: 3 mins

Total Time: 10 mins

Servings per Recipe: 1

Calories	197.8
Fat	5.7g
Cholesterol	189.2mg
Sodium	237.8mg
Carbohydrates	26.2g
Protein	8.6g

Ingredients

1 egg
1 tbsp. sugar
1 1/2 tbsp. milk
2 tbsp. flour

1/2 tsp. vanilla
1 dash salt
butter

Directions

1. In a bowl, add all the ingredients except the butter and mix until well combined.
2. In a frying pan, add the butter over low heat and cook until melted.
3. Place desired amount of the mixture and tilt the pan to spread in a thin layer.
4. Cook until golden brown from both sides.

CREPES
for Monday

Prep Time: 8 mins
Total Time: 8 mins

Servings per Recipe: 1
Calories	54.8
Fat	3.6g
Cholesterol	53.4mg
Sodium	73.1mg
Carbohydrates	3.1g
Protein	2.4g

Ingredients

3 eggs
2/3 C. milk
2 tbsp. unsalted butter, melted
1/4 tsp. salt

1/3 C. whole wheat flour

Directions

1. In a bowl, add the melted butter, milk, eggs and salt and beat until blended nicely.
2. Add the flour and beat until blended nicely.
3. With a plastic wrap, cover the bowl loosely and keep aside for about 1 1/2 hours.
4. Grease a frying pan with a little butter and heat over medium heat.
5. Place about 2 tbsp. of the mixture and tilt the pan to spread in a thin layer.
6. Cook for about 1 1/2 minutes, flipping once after 1 minute.
7. Enjoy.

Stuffed
Italian Crepes

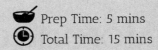

Prep Time: 5 mins
Total Time: 15 mins

Servings per Recipe: 1

Calories	75.8
Fat	1.6g
Cholesterol	24.4mg
Sodium	150.6mg
Carbohydrates	11.9g
Protein	3.0g

Ingredients

1 C. flour
1 C. milk
1 beaten egg

1/2 tsp. salt

Directions

1. In a bowl, add all the ingredients and mix until well combined.
2. Place a frying pan over medium heat until heated through.
3. Place about 1/4 C. of the mixture and tilt the pan to spread in a thin layer.
4. Cook until golden brown from both sides.
5. Repeat with the remaining mixture.
6. Enjoy.

CREPES
in Florence

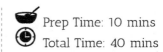 Prep Time: 10 mins

Total Time: 40 mins

Servings per Recipe: 6

Calories	475.5
Fat	27.5g
Cholesterol	219.8mg
Sodium	856.7mg
Carbohydrates	24.8g
Protein	31.4g

Ingredients

Florentine
1 lb. chicken breast, boneless, skinless, cubed
3 garlic cloves
1 (10 oz.) cans cream of chicken soup
4 oz. cheddar cheese
10 oz. spinach, chopped
1/2 C. milk
2 tbsp. butter

Parmesan cheese
salt and pepper
Crepe
1 C. flour
1 C. milk
4 eggs
1 tbsp. melted butter
1/2 tsp. salt

Directions

1. In a bowl, add the flour, butter, eggs, milk and salt and beat until well combined. Keep aside.
2. In a skillet, add the butter and cook until melted.
3. Add the chicken and garlic and stir fry for about 4-6 minutes.
4. Add the cream of chicken and milk and stir to combine.
5. Set the heat to medium-low and cook until just boiling.
6. Stir in the cheese and spinach and until the cheese is melted completely. Cook until the sauce reduces to half.
7. Meanwhile, place a lightly greased skillet over heat until heated.
8. Place about 3 tbsp. of the mixture and tilt the pan to spread in a thin layer.
9. Cook until golden brown.
10. Repeat with the remaining mixture.
11. Place about 3/4 C. of chicken mixture in the center of each crepe.
12. Wrap each crepe and enjoy with a topping of the Parmesan cheese.

Bethany
Shore Crepes

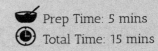

Prep Time: 5 mins
Total Time: 15 mins

Servings per Recipe: 1
Calories	298.9
Fat	16.8g
Cholesterol	400.4mg
Sodium	257.3mg
Carbohydrates	9.3g
Protein	23.1g

Ingredients

Filling
1/4 C. part-skim ricotta cheese
1 dash ground cinnamon
1 g sugar substitute
1/8-1/4 tsp. cocoa powder
Crepe
2 eggs

2 tbsp. part-skim ricotta cheese
1/2 tsp. ground cinnamon
1 1/2 tsp. vanilla extract
1 (1 g) packet sugar substitute

Directions

1. For the crepe mix: in a bowl, add the eggs and beat well.
2. Add the remaining ingredients and beat until combined nicely.
3. Place a greased crepe pan over medium heat until heated through.
4. Place desired amount of the mixture and tilt the pan to spread in a thin layer.
5. Cook until done completely from one side.
6. Meanwhile, for the filling: in a bowl, add all the ingredients and mix until well combined.
7. Carefully, change the side of the crepe and cook slightly.
8. Now, place the filling mixture on the center of crepe in a line and immediately, roll over top.
9. Cook until cooked completely.
10. Repeat with the remaining crepe mixture and filling.
11. Enjoy.

BROOKLYN
Cheesecake Crepes

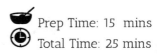 Prep Time: 15 mins

Total Time: 25 mins

Servings per Recipe: 12
Calories   108.8
Fat   4.6g
Cholesterol   43.2mg
Sodium   92.8mg
Carbohydrates   14.5g
Protein   2.9g

Ingredients

Crepe
2 eggs
1/4 C. milk
2 tbsp. water
4 tbsp. flour
1/8 tsp. sal
Filling
4 oz. cream cheese, softened
6 tbsp. cottage cheese

1/4 C. sugar
Sauce
2 C. fresh strawberries, chopped roughly
1 tbsp. lemon juice
1/3 C. sugar

Directions

1. In a bowl, add the milk, eggs and water and beat well.
2. Add the salt and flour and beat until just combined.
3. Place a lightly greased crepe pan over medium heat until heated through. Place about 2 tbsp. of the mixture and tilt the pan to spread in a thin layer.
4. Cook until golden brown from both sides.
5. Repeat with the remaining mixture.
6. For the filling: in a bowl, add the sugar, cottage cheese and cream cheese and with an electric beater, beat until smooth.
7. For the sauce: in another, add the strawberries, sugar and lemon juice and gently, toss to coat.
8. Place about 2 tbsp. of the filling into each crepe and carefully, roll it.
9. Place the crepes onto serving plates, seam side down.
10. Top each with the sauce and enjoy.

Crepes
in Slovenia

Prep Time: 15 mins
Total Time: 25 mins

Servings per Recipe: 6

Calories	145.3
Fat	5.2g
Cholesterol	72.7mg
Sodium	254.7mg
Carbohydrates	18.6g
Protein	5.6g

Ingredients

1 C. flour
2 eggs
1 C. milk
1 tsp. sugar
1 tbsp. butter, melted
1/2 tsp. salt
jam

powdered sugar
fruit syrup
whipped cream

Directions

1. In a bowl, add the sugar, flour and salt and mix well.
2. Add the eggs, one at a time, beating until well combined.
3. Add the milk and beat until smooth.
4. Add the butter and stir to combine.
5. Pour about 1/2 C. batter into a heated, lightly greased skillet.
6. Swirl around skillet to coat bottom of pan.

MEDITERRANEAN
Goat Cheese Crepes

Prep Time: 20 mins
Total Time: 48 mins

Servings per Recipe: 4

Calories	439.0
Fat	34.0g
Cholesterol	72.2mg
Sodium	605.2mg
Carbohydrates	10.2g
Protein	26.9g

Ingredients

12 (6 inch) crepes
3 tbsp. extra virgin olive oil
1 1/4 lb. mushrooms, rinsed, trimmed and thinly sliced
1/4 C. fresh flat-leaf parsley, chopped
1 tbsp. fresh thyme leave
1 garlic clove, finely chopped

salt & pepper
1 (10 oz.) packages fresh spinach, washed, stemmed & coarsely chopped
5 oz. goat cheese, crumbled
2 C. mozzarella cheese, shredded

Directions

1. Set your oven to 350 degrees F before doing anything else.
2. In a wok, add the oil over medium-high heat and cook until heated through. Stir in the mushrooms and stir fry for about 9 minutes.
3. Add the garlic, thyme, parsley, salt and pepper and stir fry for about 1 minute. Add the spinach and stir to combine.
4. Set the heat to medium and cook, covered for about 2 minutes.
5. Uncover and stir in the goat cheese until melted completely.
6. Remove from the heat.
7. Place the mushroom mixture on the center of each crepe evenly.
8. Carefully, roll each crepe.
9. In the bottom of a 13x9-inch baking dish, place the rolled crepes side by side and top with the mozzarella cheese.
10. With a piece of foil, cover the baking dish evenly.
11. Cook in the oven for about 15 minutes.
12. Remove from the oven and keep aside to cool slightly.
13. Enjoy warm.

Buttery
Orange Crepes

Prep Time: 15 mins
Total Time: 17 mins

Servings per Recipe: 9
Calories	122.3
Fat	5.2g
Cholesterol	59.4mg
Sodium	86.2mg
Carbohydrates	14.0g
Protein	4.1g

Ingredients

1 C. flour
1/8 tsp. salt
1 tbsp. sugar
1 1/2 C. warm milk
2 eggs
2 tbsp. butter, melted
1 tsp. vanilla

1/2 tsp. orange extract
2-4 tbsp. butter, softened

Directions

1. In a blender, add the flour, sugar and salt and for about 2-3 seconds.
2. Add the remaining ingredients except the softened butter and pulse for about 15 seconds.
3. Keep aside for about 18-20 minutes.
4. Grease a small frying pan with softened butter and place over medium heat until heated through.
5. Place about 1/4 C. of the mixture and tilt the pan to spread in a thin layer.
6. Cook until golden brown from both sides.
7. Repeat with the remaining mixture
8. Enjoy.

SWEET COCOA
Crepes

Prep Time: 10 mins
Total Time: 1 hr 30 mins

Servings per Recipe: 1
Calories	62.4
Fat	2.4g
Cholesterol	39.3mg
Sodium	38.8mg
Carbohydrates	7.9g
Protein	2.4g

Ingredients

3 eggs
1 C. flour
2 tbsp. sugar
2 tbsp. cocoa

1 1/4 C. buttermilk
2 tbsp. melted butter

Directions

1. In a food processor, add all the ingredients and pulse until well combined.
2. Transfer the mixture into a bowl and place in the fridge for about 1 hour.
3. Place a nonstick frying pan over medium heat until heated through.
4. Place desired amount of the mixture and tilt the pan to spread in a thin layer.
5. Cook until golden brown from both sides.
6. Repeat with the remaining mixture.
7. Enjoy.

Crepes
California

Prep Time: 30 mins
Total Time: 30 mins

Servings per Recipe: 6
Calories	660.9
Fat	43.9g
Cholesterol	207.5mg
Sodium	293.0mg
Carbohydrates	61.6g
Protein	8.4g

Ingredients

Crepes
1 C. flour
1/4 C. confectioners' sugar
2 eggs
1 C. milk
3 tbsp. butter, melted
1 tsp. vanilla
1/4 tsp. salt
Sauce
1/3-1/2 C. butter

1/2 C. packed brown sugar
3/4 tsp. cinnamon
1/4 tsp. allspice
1/2 C. half-and-half
4 -5 bananas, sliced 1/2-inch thick
Topping
1 1/2 C. whipped heavy cream
1 pinch cinnamon

Directions

1. In a bowl, sift together the powdered sugar and flour and.
2. Add the butter, milk, eggs, vanilla and salt and with a wire whisk, beat until well combined and smooth.
3. Place a lightly greased skillet over medium heat until heated through.
4. Place desired amount of the mixture and tilt the pan to spread in a thin layer.
5. Cook until golden brown from both sides.
6. Repeat with the remaining mixture.
7. Enjoy.

OLD
German Style Crepes

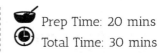

Prep Time: 20 mins
Total Time: 30 mins

Servings per Recipe: 6
Calories	307.9
Fat	13.9g
Cholesterol	137.6mg
Sodium	114.6mg
Carbohydrates	37.5g
Protein	10.0g

Ingredients

4 large eggs
1 1/2 C. milk
1 pinch salt
1 C. all-purpose flour
1 tbsp. melted unsalted butter
1/2 C. apricot jam

1 tsp. fresh lemon juice
1/2 C. walnuts, coarsely ground
confectioners' sugar, for dusting
chocolate syrup, for serving

Directions

1. In a bowl, adds 1/2 C. of the milk, eggs and salt and beat until well combined.
2. Add the flour and beat until smooth.
3. Add the butter and remaining milk and beat until a creamy mixture is formed.
4. Keep aside for about 1 hour.
5. Grease a crepe pan with the butter and place over medium heat until heated through.
6. Place about 1/4 C. of the mixture and tilt the pan to spread in a thin layer.
7. Cook for about 40 seconds, flipping once half way through.
8. Repeat with the remaining mixture.
9. Set your oven to 400 degrees F and grease a 9x13-inch baking dish.
10. In a pot, add the lemon juice and apricot jam and cook until smooth, mixing continuously.
11. Place about 1 tsp. of the jam mixture over each crepe evenly and then top with 1 tbsp. of the walnuts. Carefully, fold each crepe into quarter.
12. In the bottom of the prepared baking dish, arrange the folded crepes.
13. With a piece of the foil, cover the baking dish.
14. Cook in the oven for about 10 minutes.
15. Remove from the oven and top with the remaining walnuts.
16. Enjoy with a sifting of the confectioners' sugar alongside the chocolate sauce.

Skinny Girl
Crepes

🥣 Prep Time: 20 mins
🕐 Total Time: 50 mins

Servings per Recipe: 1

Calories	97.8
Fat	3.2g
Cholesterol	40.6mg
Sodium	97.5mg
Carbohydrates	13.8g
Protein	3.0g

Ingredients

1 C. rice flour
1/4 tsp. salt
2 eggs

1 C. milk
1 tbsp. melted margarine

Directions

1. In a bowl, add all the ingredients and with a wire whisk, beat until smooth.
2. Place a frying pan over medium-high heat until heated through.
3. Place about 1/4 C. of the mixture and tilt the pan to spread in a thin layer.
4. Cook for about 1 minute, flipping once half way through.
5. Repeat with the remaining mixture.
6. Enjoy.

BAJA
Crepes

Prep Time: 10 mins
Total Time: 40 mins

Servings per Recipe: 4

Calories	336.3
Fat	19.1g
Cholesterol	182.3mg
Sodium	343.6mg
Carbohydrates	32.1g
Protein	9.6g

Ingredients

3 eggs
1 C. milk
1 1/2 tbsp. butter, melted
3/4 C. flour, sifted
1 tbsp. sugar
1/4 tsp. salt
3 tbsp. butter, approximately

1 1/2 C. fresh blueberries
granulated sugar
powdered sugar, sifted
lemon wedge
warm melted butter

Directions

1. In a bowl, add the eggs and beat well.
2. Add 1 1/2 tbsp. of the butter and milk and beat until well combined.
3. In another bowl, sift together the flour, sugar and salt.
4. Add the flour mixture into the bowl of the egg mixture and beat until smooth.
5. Grease a frying pan with the remaining butter and place over medium heat until heated through.
6. Place about 3 tbsp. of the mixture and tilt the pan to spread in a thin layer.
7. Cook until golden brown from both sides.
8. Repeat with the remaining mixture.
9. In a bowl, add the blueberries and granulated sugar and toss to coat well.
10. Place about 3 tbsp. of the blueberries in the middle of each crepe.
11. Carefully, fold each crepe in half.
12. Sprinkle with the powdered sugar and enjoy alongside the lemon wedges and warm melted butter.

Cardamom
Crepes

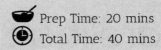 Prep Time: 20 mins
🕐 Total Time: 40 mins

Servings per Recipe: 5
Calories	247.1
Fat	6.6g
Cholesterol	115.2mg
Sodium	191.9mg
Carbohydrates	35.3g
Protein	10.3g

Ingredients

200 g flour
1 tsp. sugar
1/4 tsp. salt
1/2 tsp. ground cardamom or 1/2 tsp.
lemon peel

3 eggs
1 1/2 C. low-fat milk
1 tbsp. oil

Directions

1. In a bowl, add all the ingredients except the oil and mix until well combined and smooth.
2. Keep aside for about 20 minutes.
3. Grease a nonstick skillet with a little oil and place over medium heat until heated through.
4. Place desired amount of the mixture and tilt the pan to spread in a thin layer.
5. Cook until golden brown from both sides.
6. Repeat with the remaining mixture.
7. Enjoy warm.

NORTH
Carolina Style Crepes

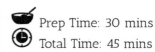

Prep Time: 30 mins
Total Time: 45 mins

Servings per Recipe: 4
Calories   495.0
Fat   34.7g
Cholesterol   179.9mg
Sodium   622.3mg
Carbohydrates   35.1g
Protein   11.1g

Ingredients

Crepe
2 eggs
1 C. Bisquick
1 C. milk
2 tbsp. butter, melted
Filling
8 oz. cream cheese

3 tbsp. sugar
1/2 tsp. vanilla extract

Directions

1. For the crepes: in a bowl, add the eggs and beat well.
2. Slowly, add the Bisquick, alternating with the milk, beating well after each addition until smooth.
3. Add the butter and beat until well combined.
4. Freeze for about 15 minutes.
5. Meanwhile, for the filling: in a bowl, add the sugar and cream cheese and with an electric mixer, beat until the sugar dissolves completely.
6. Add the vanilla extract and beat on high speed until fluffy.
7. Remove the crepe mixture from the freezer and beat slightly.
8. Place a lightly greased crepe pan over medium-low heat until heated through.
9. Place about 1/4 C. of the mixture and tilt the pan to spread in a thin layer.
10. Cook until golden brown from both sides.
11. Repeat with the remaining mixture.
12. Place the filling onto the center of each crepe evenly.
13. Carefully, fold each crepe over the filling and enjoy.

Iron
Monkey Crepes

Prep Time: 5 mins
Total Time: 35 mins

Servings per Recipe: 1
Calories	78.4
Fat	3.5g
Cholesterol	23.0mg
Sodium	48.7mg
Carbohydrates	9.7g
Protein	2.0g

Ingredients

2 eggs
1 1/4 C. milk
3 tbsp. oil
1/2 tsp. vanilla
1 very ripe banana

3 tbsp. sugar
1 C. flour
1/4 tsp. salt

Directions

1. In a food processor, add all the ingredients and pulse on high speed until well combined.
2. Place a greased frying pan over medium-low heat until heated through.
3. Place about 3 tbsp. of the mixture and tilt the pan to spread in a thin layer.
4. Cook until golden brown from both sides.
5. Repeat with the remaining mixture.
6. Enjoy warm.

AMERICAN
Dinner Crepes

Prep Time: 30 mins
Total Time: 2 hrs

Servings per Recipe: 8
Calories	571.4
Fat	40.1g
Cholesterol	181.3mg
Sodium	736.9mg
Carbohydrates	22.7g
Protein	30.6g

Ingredients

1 C. milk
2 tbsp. milk
2 eggs
2 tbsp. butter, melted
1 C. all-purpose flour
1/4 tsp. salt
Filling
1/4 C. butter
1/4 C. all-purpose flour
2 C. chicken broth

2 tsp. Worcestershire sauce
3 C. cheddar cheese, shredded, divided
2 C. sour cream
2 (9 oz.) packages frozen broccoli spears, cooked and drained
2 1/2 C. cooked chicken, cubed

Directions

1. In a bowl, add the flour and salt and mix well.
2. In a bowl, add the butter, eggs and milk and beat until well combined.
3. Add the flour mixture and beat until well combined and smooth.
4. Cover the bowl and place in the fridge for about 1 hour.
5. Place a lightly greased frying pan over medium-high heat until heated through.
6. Place about 1/4 C. of the mixture and tilt the pan to spread in a thin layer.
7. Cook until golden brown from both sides.
8. Repeat with the remaining mixture.
9. Set your oven to 350 degrees F and grease a 13x9x2-inch baking dish.
10. Meanwhile, in a pot, add the butter and cook until melted.
11. Add the flour and cook until smooth, mixing continuously.
12. Stir in the broth and Worcestershire sauce and cook until boiling.
13. Cook for about 2 minutes, mixing continuously.

14. Set the heat to low.
15. Add 2 C. of the cheese and stir to combine.
16. Cook for about 10 minutes, mixing frequently.
17. Remove from the heat and stir in the sour cream until well combined and smooth.
18. Put the chicken and broccoli onto each crepe evenly and top with 1/3 C. of the cheese sauce.
19. Carefully, fold each crepe over the filling.
20. In the bottom of the prepared baking dish, arrange the crepes, seam side down and top with the remaining cheese sauce evenly, followed by the remaining cheddar cheese.
21. Cook in the oven for about 20 minutes.
22. Enjoy hot.

HUBBY'S
Favorite Crepes

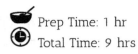
Prep Time: 1 hr
Total Time: 9 hrs

Servings per Recipe: 1
Calories	55.9
Fat	2.5g
Cholesterol	18.6mg
Sodium	97.2mg
Carbohydrates	6.6g
Protein	1.4g

Ingredients

3/4 C. sourdough starter, at room temperature
1 C. 100°C warm water
1 1/4 C. all-purpose flour
2 eggs, at room temperature
3 tbsp. salad oil
1/2 tsp. salt

1/2 tsp. baking soda
1 tbsp. sugar
butter

Directions

1. In a bowl, add the flour, starter and water and flour mix until well combined and smooth.
2. Cover the bowl and place in a warm area for about 8 hours.
3. In another bowl, add the oil and eggs and beat well.
4. Add the oil mixture into the bowl of the starter mixture and mix well.
5. In a third bowl, add the sugar, baking soda and salt and mix well.
6. Add the sugar mixture into the bowl of the starter mixture and mix until well combined.
7. With a plastic wrap, cover the bowl lightly and keep aside at room temperature for about 15 minutes.
8. In a crepe pan, add 1/4 tsp. of the butter over medium heat and cook until melted.
9. Place about 2 tbsp. of the mixture and tilt the pan to spread in a thin layer.
10. Cook until golden brown from both sides.
11. Repeat with the remaining mixture.
12. Enjoy warm.

Shrimp
Crepes

Prep Time: 20 mins
Total Time: 50 mins

Servings per Recipe: 4
Calories   445.3
Fat   24.4g
Cholesterol   384.4mg
Sodium   578.9mg
Carbohydrates   19.8g
Protein   35.0g

Ingredients

Crepes
1/2 C. flour
1 pinch salt
1 - 2 egg
1/2 C. milk
2 tbsp. butter, melted
2 - 4 tbsp. chopped fresh herbs
Filling
2 tbsp. butter
2 tbsp. flour
1 C. milk

1 egg yolk
2 tbsp. cream
1 pinch allspice
1 pinch salt
1 pinch white pepper
4 tbsp. grated Parmesan cheese
4 tbsp. grated gruyere, divided
1 lb. cooked shrimp

Directions

1. For the crepes: in a bowl, add the flour and salt and mix well.
2. Add the milk and eggs and beat until smooth.
3. Add the herbs and butter and stir to combine well.
4. Keep aside for about 30 minutes.
5. Now, stir the mixture well.
6. Place a lightly greased crepe pan over medium heat until heated through.
7. Place desired amount of the mixture and tilt the pan to spread in a thin layer.
8. Cook until golden brown from both sides.
9. Repeat with the remaining mixture.
10. For the sauce: in a pot, add the butter over medium heat and cook until melted.
11. Stir in the flour and cook until smooth, mixing continuously.
12. Add the milk and cook until desired thickness, mixing continuously.

13. In a bowl, add the cream and egg yolk and beat until well combined.
14. Place a little of the hot sauce into the cream mixture and mix until well combined.
15. Add the cream mixture into the pan of the sauce mixture and stir to combine.
16. Add the allspice, salt and pepper and stir to combine.
17. Add 2 tbsp. of each Gruyere and Parmesan and stir to combine well.
18. Stir in the cooked seafood and cook until heated completely.
19. Set the broiler of your oven.
20. Place the seafood mixture onto the center of each crepe evenly.
21. Carefully, roll crepe and arrange onto a baking sheet.
22. Place a little sauce from the seafood mixture over the crepes, followed by the remaining cheeses.
23. Cook under the broiler until top becomes golden brown.
24. Enjoy hot.

Eastern
European Crepes

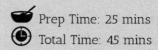 Prep Time: 25 mins
Total Time: 45 mins

Servings per Recipe: 1
Calories   81.7
Fat   5.2g
Cholesterol   55.1mg
Sodium   165.4mg
Carbohydrates   4.8g
Protein   3.8g

Ingredients

Crepe
4 large eggs
1 C. whole milk, homogenized
6 tbsp. cold water
1 C. all-purpose flour
1/2 tsp. salt
Filling
2 C. cottage cheese
2 large egg yolks

2 tbsp. whipping cream
1/4 tsp. salt
1 tsp. chopped fresh dill weed
1/8 C. butter (for greasing)
1/4 C. butter, for dotting

Directions

1. Set your oven to 250 degrees F before doing anything else.
2. In a bowl, add the eggs and with a hand held electric mixer, beat until fluffy and light.
3. Add the flour, milk, water and salt and beat until well combined and smooth.
4. Place a lightly greased crepe pan over medium heat until heated through.
5. Place desired amount of the mixture and tilt the pan to spread in a thin layer.
6. Cook for about 1 minute.
7. Transfer the cooked crepe onto an oven-proof plate.
8. Repeat with the remaining mixture.
9. Place the plate into the oven to keep warm.
10. For the filling: in a cheese cloth, place the cottage cheese and with your hands, squeeze to release the moisture.
11. In a bowl, add the cottage cheese, whipping cream, egg yolks, dill weed and salt and mix until well combined.
12. Remove the plate of warmed crepes from the oven.

13. Now, set your oven to 350 degrees F and lightly, grease a 13x9-inch oven proof casserole dish with the butter.
14. Arrange the cooked crepes onto a smooth surface, browned side down.
15. Place about 1 heaping tbsp. of the cheese mixture onto one edge of each crepe close to the edge.
16. Carefully, roll each crepe over the filling and tuck in each side to secure the filling.
17. In the bottom of the prepared casserole dish, arrange the rolled crepes in layers and top with 1/4 C. of the butter in the form of dots.
18. Cook in the oven for about 20 minutes.
19. Enjoy hot.

Hot
Spanish Chicken Crepes

Prep Time: 45 mins
Total Time: 6 hrs 45 mins

Servings per Recipe: 6	
Calories	367.7
Fat	14.5g
Cholesterol	188.8mg
Sodium	295.6mg
Carbohydrates	10.1g
Protein	47.6g

Ingredients

3 lb. skinless chicken thighs, bone in
1 tbsp. olive oil
1 C. grape tomatoes
3 garlic cloves, thinly sliced
1/2 medium yellow onion, rough chopped
1 medium jalapeño pepper, seeded and rough chopped
1/4 tsp. ground cumin
1/8 tsp. ground allspice
1/4 tsp. whole cloves
1 tbsp. chili powder
1 cinnamon stick, 2 1/2 to 3 inches
1/2 C. chicken stock
2 tbsp. peanut butter

1/3 C. fresh blueberries
1/4 C. brewed coffee
2 tbsp. sugar-free chocolate syrup
1/4 C. orange juice
1/2 tsp. Splenda granular
1 slice bread, torn into pieces
salt
pepper
12 -16 prepared crepes
light sour cream
4 -5 scallions, sliced

Directions

1. Set your oven to 375 degrees F before doing anything else.

2. In the bottom of an 8x8-inch baking dish, place the onions, tomatoes, jalapeño, garlic, salt, pepper and a little oil and toss to coat well.

3. Cook in the oven for about 10 minutes.

4. Meanwhile, in a frying pan, place the cinnamon stick, cloves, cumin, ground allspice and chili powder and stir fry until aromatic.

5. Remove the tomato mixture from the oven and keep aside to cool slightly.

6. For the mole sauce: in a food processor, add the tomato mixture toasted spices, blueberries, bread, peanut butter, chocolate syrup, coffee, orange juice, stock and Splenda and pulse until well combined and smooth.

7. In the bottom of a crock pot, place the chicken and top with the mole sauce evenly.
8. Set the crock pot on Low and cook, covered for about 6-8 hours.
9. Uncover the crock pot and transfer the chicken thighs onto a plate.
10. Remove the meat from the bones and with 2 forks, shred it.
11. Transfer the mole sauce into a pot over medium-high heat and cook until boiling.
12. Set the heat to low and cook for about 18-20 minutes.
13. Arrange the crepes onto a smooth surface.
14. Place the shredded chicken onto the center of each crepe evenly.
15. Carefully, fold each crepe over the filling.
16. Divide the crepes onto serving plates and place the mole sauce over each serving evenly.
17. Enjoy with a topping of the sour cream and scallions.

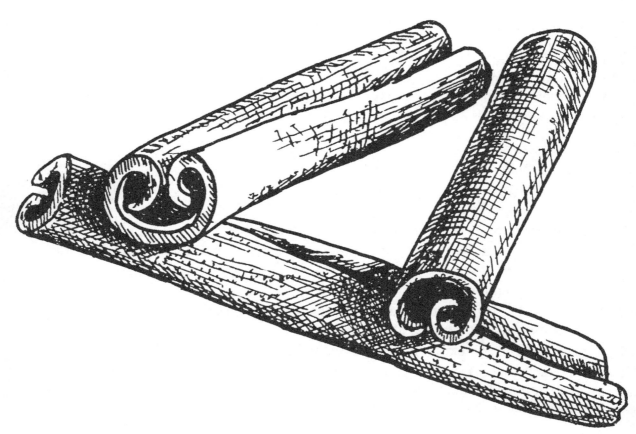

Ginger
Sesame Crepes

Prep Time: 10 mins
Total Time: 40 mins

Servings per Recipe: 60	
Calories	15.5
Fat	1.3g
Cholesterol	20.7mg
Sodium	14.5mg
Carbohydrates	0.1g
Protein	0.6g

Ingredients

1/4 C. butter, melted
1 tbsp. ginger, finely minced
6 eggs
1/3 C. low-fat milk

1 tsp. sesame oil
salt

Directions

1. In a bowl, add the eggs, 2 tbsp. of the butter, sesame oil, milk, ginger and salt and beat until well combined.
2. Grease a crepe pan with a little of the remaining butter and place over medium heat until heated through.
3. Place desired amount of the mixture and tilt the pan to spread in a thin layer.
4. Cook until golden brown from both sides.
5. Repeat with the remaining mixture.
6. Enjoy.

FRUITY
Cottage Crepes

Prep Time: 20 mins
Total Time: 40 mins

Servings per Recipe: 18
Calories	188.9
Fat	7.5g
Cholesterol	73.9mg
Sodium	134.9mg
Carbohydrates	23.3g
Protein	8.2g

Ingredients

4 eggs
1 C. flour
1 C. milk
1 tbsp. light brown sugar
1/4 tsp. almond extract
1 (16 oz.) containers cottage cheese
2 egg yolks
3 tbsp. sugar
1/2 C. sugar
1 tbsp. orange zest

1/2 C. chopped blanched almond
2 tbsp. cornstarch
2/3 C. orange juice
4 C. blueberries
1/2 C. toasted sliced natural almonds

Directions

1. Set your oven to 300 degrees F before doing anything else and lightly, grease a baking sheet.
2. In a bowl, add the milk, eggs, flour, brown sugar and almond extract and beat until well combined and smooth.
3. Place a greased frying pan over medium heat until heated through.
4. Place about 3 tbsp. of the mixture and tilt the pan to spread in a thin layer.
5. Cook until golden brown from both sides.
6. Repeat with the remaining mixture.
7. Meanwhile, for the filling: in a food processor, add the egg yolks, cottage cheese, 3 tbsp. of the sugar and orange peel and pulse until blended nicely.
8. Transfer the mixture into a bowl.
9. Add the almonds and stir until well combined and smooth.
10. Keep aside until using.
11. For the blueberry sauce: in a pot, add the orange juice, blueberries, cornstarch and

remaining 1/2 C. of the sugar over medium-high heat and cook until boiling, mixing continuously.

12. Cook for about 1 minute, mixing continuously.
13. Place about 2 round tbsp. of the filling mixture onto each crepe.
14. Carefully, roll each crepe.
15. In the bottom of the prepared baking sheet, arrange the crepes.
16. Cook in the oven for about 15 minutes.
17. Enjoy with a topping of the blueberry sauce and almonds.

MINIMAL
Crepes

Prep Time: 1 hr
Total Time: 1 hr 40 mins

Servings per Recipe: 1
Calories   131.8
Fat   2.5g
Cholesterol   59.2mg
Sodium   33.8mg
Carbohydrates   20.4g
Protein   5.2g

Ingredients

500 -600 g flour   500 ml milk
6 eggs
2 tbsp. vanilla

Directions

1. In a bowl, add all the ingredients and beat until well combined.
2. Place in the fridge for about 1 hour.
3. Place a greased frying pan over medium heat until heated through.
4. Place about 1/3 C. of the mixture and tilt the pan to spread in a thin layer.
5. Cook for about 2 1/2 minutes, flipping once after 1 1/2 minutes.
6. Repeat with the remaining mixture.
7. Enjoy.

Fresh
Summer Crepes

Prep Time: 10 mins
Total Time: 30 mins

Servings per Recipe: 4
Calories	266.2
Fat	11.5g
Cholesterol	119.3mg
Sodium	146.1mg
Carbohydrates	31.8g
Protein	9.3g

Ingredients

105 g plain flour
2 eggs
2 lemons juice
1/2 tsp. sugar

1/8 tsp. salt
300 ml milk
30 g unsalted butter, melted

Directions

1. In a bowl, place the flour and then, make a well in the center.
2. In the well, add the egg, 1 at a time and with a wooden spoon, mix until well combined.
3. Add the sugar, salt and lemon zest and mix well.
4. Slowly, add the milk and beat until well combined and smooth.
5. Keep aside for about 1 1/2 hours.
6. Add the melted butter and beat until well combined and smooth.
7. Place a lightly greased crepe pan over medium heat until heated through.
8. Place desired amount of the mixture and tilt the pan to spread in a thin layer.
9. Cook until golden brown from both sides.
10. Repeat with the remaining mixture.
11. Fold each crepe in triangle and enjoy with a drizzling of the lemon juice.

6-INGREDIENT
American Crepes

Prep Time: 5 mins
Total Time: 1 hr 35 mins

Servings per Recipe: 4
Calories	184.2
Fat	4.5g
Cholesterol	97.2mg
Sodium	55.6mg
Carbohydrates	28.7g
Protein	8.7g

Ingredients

1/4 C. all-purpose flour
1 C. buckwheat flour
2 eggs
1/2 C. milk

1 C. water
butter, for frying

Directions

1. In a bowl, add all the ingredients except the butter and beat until well combined and smooth.
2. Keep aside for about 1 hour.
3. In a frying pan, add a little butter over medium heat and cook until melted.
4. Place about 1/4 C. of the mixture and tilt the pan to spread in a thin layer.
5. Cook for about 2 minutes, flipping once after 1 1/2 minutes.
6. Repeat with the remaining mixture.
7. Enjoy.

Simple
Crepe Formula

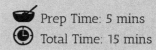 Prep Time: 5 mins
Total Time: 15 mins

Servings per Recipe: 1
Calories	117.6
Fat	2.4g
Cholesterol	50.7mg
Sodium	178.4mg
Carbohydrates	19.4g
Protein	4.1g

Ingredients

1/2 C. flour
3 tbsp. powdered sugar
1/4 tsp. salt
1/2 C. milk

1 egg
vegetable oil

Directions

1. In a bowl, add the flour, salt and powdered and mix well.
2. Add the eggs and milk and beat until smooth.
3. In a frying pan, add the oil over medium heat and cook until heated through.
4. Place about 1/4 of the mixture and tilt the pan to spread in a thin layer.
5. Cook until golden brown from both sides.
6. Repeat with the remaining mixture.
7. Enjoy.

HEALTHIER
Alternative Crepes

 Prep Time: 3 mins
🕐 Total Time: 6 mins

Servings per Recipe: 1
Calories	162.2
Fat	4.3g
Cholesterol	1.2mg
Sodium	378.0mg
Carbohydrates	12.7g
Protein	16.6g

Ingredients

1/2 C. fat free egg substitute
2 tbsp. flour
2 tbsp. water
1 (1 g) packet artificial sweetener

1 pinch salt

Directions

1. In a bowl, add all the ingredients and beat until well combined.
2. Place a lightly greased frying pan over medium-high heat until heated through.
3. Place the mixture and tilt the pan to spread in a thin layer.
4. Cook until golden brown from both sides.
5. Enjoy.

Simply
Sweet Crepes

Prep Time: 20 mins
Total Time: 20 mins

Servings per Recipe: 2
Calories	363.4
Fat	13.4g
Cholesterol	301.7mg
Sodium	264.5mg
Carbohydrates	40.0g
Protein	19.0g

Ingredients

1 1/3 C. milk
2/3 C. flour
3 eggs
1 pinch salt

1 pinch granulated sugar

Directions

1. In a bowl, add all the ingredients and mix until well combined.
2. Place a lightly greased crepe pan over medium heat until heated through.
3. Place desired amount of the mixture and tilt the pan to spread in a thin layer.
4. Cook until golden brown from both sides.
5. Repeat with the remaining mixture.
6. Enjoy.

LASAGNA
Crepes

Prep Time: 40 mins
Total Time: 1 hr 40 mins

Servings per Recipe: 6
Calories   848.4
Fat   41.5g
Cholesterol   268.5mg
Sodium   1828.6mg
Carbohydrates   77.0g
Protein   40.0g

Ingredients

Crepes
3 eggs
1 C. water
1 1/2 C. all-purpose flour
nonstick Pam cooking spray
Filling
2 lb. whole milk ricotta cheese
1/2 C. Pecorino Romano cheese, freshly grated

1 C. shredded whole milk mozzarella
3 tbsp. fresh basil, chopped
4 tbsp. fresh parsley, chopped
2 eggs, beaten
1/2 tsp. fresh ground pepper
Other
2 quarts marinara sauce
1 C. shredded mozzarella cheese

Directions

1. For the crepes: in a bowl, add the water and eggs and beat well.
2. Slowly, add the flour and beat until smooth.
3. Place in the fridge for about 30 minutes.
4. Meanwhile, for the filling: in a bowl, add the eggs, Ricotta, Mozzarella, Pecorino Romano cheese, parsley, basil and pepper and mix until well combined.
5. Cover the bowl and place in the fridge for about 30 minutes.
6. Place about 1/3 C. of the mixture and tilt the pan to spread in a thin layer.
7. Cook for about 1 minute.
8. Flip and cook for about 5 seconds more.
9. Repeat with the remaining mixture.
10. Transfer the crepes onto a smooth surface and let them cool.
11. Set your oven to 325 degrees F.
12. Place 2 tbsp. of the filling mixture onto the center of each crepe.
13. Carefully, roll each crepe.

14. In the bottom of a 13x9-inch baking dish, place a layer of the marinara sauce and arrange 1 layer of the crepes on top, seam side down.
15. Repeat the layers, ending with a layer of the marinara sauce.
16. With a piece of the foil, cover the baking dish and cook in the oven for about 40 minutes.
17. Remove the foil and top with the remaining Mozzarella cheese evenly.
18. Cook in the oven for about 5-10 minutes.
19. Remove from the oven and keep aside for about 9-10 minutes.
20. Enjoy.

FRIENDSHIP
Crepes

 Prep Time: 30 mins
Total Time: 1 hr

Servings per Recipe: 4
Calories	758.6
Fat	32.2g
Cholesterol	219.0mg
Sodium	338.9mg
Carbohydrates	101.6g
Protein	17.4g

Ingredients

280 g all-purpose flour
120 g sugar
90 g butter, unsalted, softened
1/2 liter milk
1 pinch salt
300 g Quark
50 g raisins

1 lemon, grated zest of
1/8 liter sour cream
powdered sugar
3 eggs

Directions

1. Set your oven to 350 degrees F before doing anything else and grease a baking dish. For the crepe mixture: in a bowl, add 1/2 of the butter, 1 egg, milk and salt and with an electric mixer, beat on medium speed for about 1 minute. Slowly, add the flour and beat on low speed for about 1 minute. Cover the bowl and place in the fridge for about 1 hour.

2. Place a lightly greased crepe pan over medium heat until heated through. Place desired amount of the mixture and tilt the pan to spread in a thin layer. Cook for about 1 1/2 minutes, flipping once half way through. Repeat with the remaining mixture.

3. For the filling: separate the remaining 2 eggs.

4. In a bowl, add the sour cream, Quark, remaining sugar, raisins, 2 egg yolks and lemon rind and beat until well combined.

5. In a clean glass bowl, add the egg whites and beat until stiff peaks form. Gently, fold the whipped egg whites into the cream mixture.

6. Place about 2-3 tsp. of the cream filling onto each crepe.

7. Carefully, roll each crepe. In the prepared baking dish, arrange the crepes. Cook in the oven for about 5-6 minutes.

8. Enjoy with a dusting of the powdered sugar.

Raspberry
Crepes

Prep Time: 10 mins
Total Time: 40 mins

Servings per Recipe: 12
Calories   180.7
Fat   5.0g
Cholesterol   72.7mg
Sodium   61.1mg
Carbohydrates   30.1g
Protein   4.1g

Ingredients

Filling
3/4 C. sugar
1/2 C. flour
2 C. milk
4 eggs
2 tbsp. butter
1 tsp. vanilla

Sauce
1 (10 oz.) packages frozen raspberries, thawed
1/4 C. sugar
2 tbsp. cornstarch
12 pre-made crepes

Directions

1. For the filling: in a pot, add the milk, flour and sugar and mix well.
2. Place the pan over low heat and cook until thick, mixing continuously. Meanwhile, in a bowl, add the eggs and beat well.
3. Add a small amount of the hot milk mixture into the bowl of beaten eggs and mix well. Place the egg mixture into the pan of the remaining milk mixture and stir to combine well.
4. Cook for about 2 minutes, mixing continuously.
5. Add the butter and vanilla and stir to combine.
6. Remove from the heat and keep aside to cool.
7. For the sauce: in a pan, place the raspberries and cook until heated completely.
8. Stir in the cornstarch and sugar and cook until thick mixing continuously.
9. Remove from the heat and keep aside to cool slightly.
10. Place a spoonful of the filing mixture onto each crepe.
11. Carefully, fold each crepe over the filling.
12. Enjoy the crepes with a topping of the warm sauce.

MIDWESTERN
Apple Crepes

Prep Time: 30 mins
Total Time: 55 mins

Servings per Recipe: 6
Calories	363.8
Fat	14.7g
Cholesterol	126.9mg
Sodium	348.3mg
Carbohydrates	54.2g
Protein	7.3g

Ingredients

2 tbsp. butter, melted
1 1/2 C. milk
2/3 C. flour
1/2 tsp. salt
3 eggs
8 apples, cored, peeled and sliced
3 tbsp. butter

3 tbsp. brown sugar
1 tsp. cinnamon
1 pinch allspice

Directions

1. In a bowl, add the eggs, milk, melted butter, flour and salt and beat until smooth.
2. Keep aside for about 2 hours.
3. In a pot, add the apple, 3 tbsp. of the butter, brown sugar, cinnamon and allspice over medium-low heat and cook until apple becomes soft, mixing occasionally.
4. Set the heat to very low to keep the apple mixture warm.
5. Place a lightly greased frying pan over medium heat until heated through.
6. Place about 1/4 C. of the mixture and tilt the pan to spread in a thin layer.
7. Cook for about 2 1/2 minutes, flipping once half way through.
8. Repeat with the remaining mixture.
9. Arrange the crepes onto a smooth surface.
10. Place about 2-3 tbsp. of the apple filling onto the center of each crepe.
11. Carefully, roll each crepe to secure the filling.
12. Enjoy warm.

Lemon
Curd Crepes

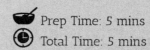

Prep Time: 5 mins
Total Time: 5 mins

Servings per Recipe: 16
Calories   50.9
Fat   1.8g
Cholesterol   7.1mg
Sodium   153.6mg
Carbohydrates   3.8g
Protein   4.6g

Ingredients

3 C. small curd cottage cheese
3 tbsp. sugar
1 tsp. grated lemon peel

1/2 tsp. vanilla

Directions

1. In a bowl, add all the ingredients and mix until well combined.
2. Place the filing into the prepared crepes and enjoy.

VERSATILE
Crepe Mix

Prep Time: 1 hr 10 mins
Total Time: 1 hr 20 mins

Servings per Recipe: 4
Calories   380.9
Fat   12.4g
Cholesterol   164.6mg
Sodium   462.3mg
Carbohydrates   50.3g
Protein   14.2g

Ingredients

3 eggs
2 C. low-fat milk
2 1/2 tsp. vanilla extract
1 2/3 C. plain flour
1/2 tsp. salt

1 1/4 tbsp. sugar
2 1/2 tbsp. butter, melted

Directions

1. In a bowl, add the flour, sugar and salt and mix well.
2. Now, sift the flour mixture into another bowl.
3. In a third bowl, add the eggs and beat well.
4. Add the milk and vanilla essence and with an electric mixer, beat until well combined.
5. Slowly, add the flour mixture and mix well.
6. Add the butter and beat until well combined.
7. Keep aside for about 1 1/2 hours.
8. Place a nonstick frying pan over medium heat until heated through.
9. Place about 2 tbsp. of the mixture and tilt the pan to spread in a thin layer.
10. Cook until golden brown from both sides.
11. Repeat with the remaining mixture.
12. Enjoy.

Ruby's
Pastoral Rhubarb Crepes

Prep Time: 1 hr
Total Time: 1 hr 15 mins

Servings per Recipe: 4
Calories	305.8
Fat	9.4g
Cholesterol	125.8mg
Sodium	385.8mg
Carbohydrates	48.9g
Protein	7.8g

Ingredients

Crepes
2 eggs
1/2 C. low-fat milk
1/2 tsp. salt
1 tsp. sugar
1/2 C. flour
1 tbsp. butter
Stuffing
1 C. blueberries
1 tbsp. maple syrup

1/2 C. light sour cream
Compote
2 C. fresh rhubarb
2 tbsp. frozen orange juice concentrate
1/4 C. sugar
1 tbsp. cornstarch
Toppings
1 tbsp. orange marmalade
4 fresh mint leaves

Directions

1. In a bowl, add the milk and eggs and beat until well combined.
2. Add the flour, sugar and salt and beat until well combined.
3. Keep aside for about 30 minutes. In a nonstick skillet, add 1/2 tsp. of the butter over medium heat and cook until melted.
4. Place about tbsp. of the mixture and tilt the pan to spread in a thin layer. Cook until golden brown from both sides. Repeat with the remaining mixture.
5. For the stuffing: in a bowl, add the blueberries, sour cream and maple sugar and gently, stir to combine.
6. For the rhubarb compote: in a pot, add the rhubarb, sugar, cornstarch and orange juice concentrate and cook until desired thickness of the mixture, mixing frequently.
7. Arrange the crepes onto a smooth surface.
8. Spread the marmalade onto each crepe evenly.
9. Place the blueberry filling onto the center of each crepe evenly.Carefully, roll each crepe.
10. Top the crepes with rhubarb compote and enjoy with a garnishing of the mint.

ALASKAN
Layered Crepes

Prep Time: 15 mins
Total Time: 1 hr 15 mins

Servings per Recipe: 24	
Calories	116.6
Fat	8.3g
Cholesterol	48.0mg
Sodium	207.5mg
Carbohydrates	5.8g
Protein	4.5

Ingredients

Crepes
1 C. flour
3 eggs
1 tsp. salt
1 1/2 C. milk
3 tbsp. butter, melted and cooled
Seafood Layer
1 (7 oz.) cans salmon, boneless skinless
1/4 C. mayonnaise

1 tbsp. chopped chives
pepper
Cheese Layer
6 oz. cream cheese, softened
2 tbsp. mayonnaise
4 slices turkey bacon, cooked crumbled

Directions

1. For the crepes: in a bowl, add the flour and salt and mix well.
2. Add the butter, eggs and milk and with a hand mixer, beat until very smooth. Keep aside for about 30 minutes.
3. Place a lightly greased crepe pan over medium heat until heated through. Place desired amount of the mixture and tilt the pan to spread in a thin layer. Cook until golden brown from both sides.
4. Repeat with the remaining mixture.
5. Keep the all 14 cooked crepes aside to cool completely.
6. After cooling, trim each crepe into a 6-inch diameter.
7. For the salmon layer: in a bowl, add the salmon, chives, 1/4 C. of the mayonnaise and pepper and with a fork, mash until well combined and smooth.
8. For the cream cheese layer: in a bowl, add the cream cheese, 2 tbsp. of the mayonnaise and bacon and mix until smooth.
9. Arrange 2 crepes onto a cutting board.
10. Place about 1/6 of the salmon mixture onto each crepe evenly.

11. Place another 2 crepes over the salmon mixture.
12. Place about 1/6 of the cream cheese over the crepes.
13. Repeat the layers in the same way to have two stacks.
14. With a plastic wrap, wrap each stack and place in the fridge for about 1 1/2 hours.
15. Cut each stack into 12 equal sized wedges and enjoy.

CREPES
in College

Prep Time: 15 mins
Total Time: 25 mins

Servings per Recipe: 6
Calories   233.6
Fat   10.9g
Cholesterol   46.4mg
Sodium   68.1mg
Carbohydrates   33.2g
Protein   2.8g

Ingredients

1 (21 oz.) cans apple pie filling
1/2 C. coarsely chopped pecans
1/2 tsp. ground cinnamon
12 prepared 7 inches crepes
1 egg, beaten

3/4 C. half-and-half cream
2 tbsp. sugar
1/2 tsp. vanilla extract
1/4 tsp. almond extract

Directions

1. Set your oven to 375 degrees F before doing anything else and grease a 13x9x2-inch baking dish.
2. In a bowl, add the pecans, pie filling and cinnamon and stir to combine well.
3. Place about 2 round tbsp. of the mixture onto the center of each crepe.
4. Carefully, roll each crepe tightly.
5. In the bottom of the prepared baking dish, arrange the rolled crepes.
6. Cook in the oven for about 10-14 minutes.
7. Meanwhile, in a microwave-safe bowl, add the sugar, cream, egg and both extracts and stir to combine.
8. Microwave, covered on power for about 5-6 minutes, stirring after every 2 minutes.
9. Remove from the microwave and keep aside to cool.
10. Enjoy the crepes with a topping of the cream mixture.

Marty's
Secret Crepes

🥣 Prep Time: 20 mins
🕐 Total Time: 40 mins

Servings per Recipe: 4
Calories	259.6
Fat	20.5g
Cholesterol	60.1mg
Sodium	553.2mg
Carbohydrates	13.6g
Protein	6.6g

Ingredients

1 small cauliflower, broken into florets
3 tbsp. butter
3 tbsp. flour
1/2 C. light cream
1/2 C. milk
1/2 tsp. salt
8 cooked crepes

1/2 C. soft breadcrumbs
1 tbsp. melted butter
1/4 C. grated Parmesan cheese

Directions

1. Set your oven to 350 degrees F before doing anything else.
2. In a steamer, place the cauliflower and steam until desired doneness. Drain the cauliflower completely.
3. For the roux: in a skillet, add 2 tbsp. of the butter and cook until melted. Add the flour, beating continuously until smooth.
4. Add the milk, cream and salt and stir to combine.
5. Set the heat to low and cook until desired thickness, mixing continuously.
6. Remove from the heat and stir in the cauliflower.
7. Fill each crepe with the cauliflower mixture evenly.
8. Carefully, fold each crepe in half.
9. In a frying pan, add the remaining butter and cook until melted completely.
10. Add the cheese and bread crumbs and stir to combine.
11. In the bottom of a shallow baking dish, arrange the rolled crepes and top with the cheese mixture evenly.
12. Cook in oven about 15-20 minutes.
13. Enjoy warm.

NEW HAMPSHIRE
Salmon Crepes

Prep Time: 20 mins
Total Time: 30 mins

Servings per Recipe: 4
Calories   281.2
Fat   23.4g
Cholesterol   222.9mg
Sodium   512.8mg
Carbohydrates   4.7g
Protein   13.1g

Ingredients

1 tbsp. chopped onion
2 tbsp. butter
1 tbsp. flour
1 C. light cream
4 oz. smoked salmon, diced
3 hard-cooked eggs, chopped
2 tbsp. capers

1/2 tsp. chopped fresh dill
1/2 tsp. fresh lemon juice
salt and black pepper
8 warm crepes
2 tbsp. grated Parmesan cheese

Directions

1. Set your oven to 400 degrees F before doing anything else and grease a baking dish.
2. For the filling: in a wok, add 1 tbsp. of the butter and cook until melted. Add the onion and stir fry for about 4-5 minutes.
3. Add the flour and stir to combine.
4. Slowly, add the cream, mixing continuously.
5. Cook for about 3-4 minutes, mixing frequently.
6. Add the eggs, salmon, dill, capers, lemon juice, salt and black pepper and stir to combine.
7. Remove from the heat.
8. Place the filling onto the center of each crepe evenly.
9. Carefully, roll each crepe.
10. In the bottom of the prepared baking dish, arrange the rolled crepes and top with the Parmesan cheese evenly, followed by the butter in the shape of dots.
11. Cook in the oven for about 5-8 minutes.
12. Enjoy warm.

Experimental
Crepes

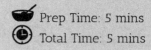

Prep Time: 5 mins
Total Time: 5 mins

Servings per Recipe: 1
Calories	117.9
Fat	9.2g
Cholesterol	186.3mg
Sodium	77.4mg
Carbohydrates	1.1g
Protein	6.7g

Ingredients

1 large egg
1 tbsp. nonfat milk
1 tsp. olive oil

1/8 tsp. Splenda sugar substitute
1/8 tsp. vanilla

Directions

1. In a bowl, add all the ingredients and beat until well combined and frothy.
2. Place a frying pan over medium-high heat until heated through.
3. Place about 1/8 C. of the mixture and tilt the pan to spread in a thin layer.
4. Cook until golden brown from both sides.
5. Repeat with the remaining mixture.
6. Enjoy.

TOPPED
Breakfast Crepes

Prep Time: 25 mins
Total Time: 1 hr 10 mins

Servings per Recipe: 4
Calories	769.9
Fat	42.9g
Cholesterol	523.4mg
Sodium	989.9mg
Carbohydrates	64.4g
Protein	32.4g

Ingredients

Crepes
4 eggs
1/4 tsp. salt
2 C. flour
2 1/2 C. milk
1/4 C. melted butter
Salsa
1 medium zucchini, cut in 1/4-inch slices
1 tsp. olive oil
1/2 sweet red pepper, diced 1/4-inch dice
2 Roma tomatoes, seeded & chopped
1/3 C. fresh coriander, chopped
1/3 C. tomato juice
1/4 tsp. ground coriander

1 tbsp. fresh lime juice
1/4 tsp. dry cumin
1/4 tsp. Worcestershire sauce
1/4 tsp. hot pepper sauce
salt and pepper
Filling
1/4 C. fresh tomato, seeded, finely chopped
2 tbsp. butter
2 C. mushrooms, thinly sliced
2 C. new fresh spinach, finely shredded
4 eggs, beaten
1 C. feta cheese, crumbled

Directions

1. Meanwhile, for the salsa: coat the zucchini slices with the oil evenly.
2. Place a lightly greased skillet over medium heat until heated through.
3. Add the zucchini slices and cook until golden brown from both sides.
4. Remove from the heat and transfer the zucchini slices into a bowl with the remaining mixture and toss to coat well.
5. Cover the bowl and place in the fridge for up to 2 hours.
6. For the crepes: in a food processor, add all the ingredients and pulse until smooth.
7. Place in the fridge for about 1 hour.

8. For the tomato sauce: in a pan, add the tomatoes over low heat and cook until heated completely, mixing often.
9. Remove from the heat and keep side, covered to keep warm.
10. In a skillet, add 1 tbsp. of the butter and cook until melted.
11. Add the mushrooms and stir fry for about 7-8 minutes.
12. With slotted spoon, transfer the spinach onto a plate.
13. In the same skillet, add the spinach and cook, covered for about 3-4 minutes.
14. Remove from the heat and stir in cooked mushrooms.
15. Cover the pan to keep the mixture warm.
16. In another skillet, add the remaining butter and cook until melted.
17. Add the eggs and cook until desired doneness of the eggs, stirring continuously.
18. Place a lightly greased crepe pan over medium heat until heated through.
19. Place desired amount of the mixture and tilt the pan to spread in a thin layer.
20. Cook until golden brown from both sides.
21. Repeat with the remaining mixture.
22. Arrange the crepes onto a smooth surface.
23. Place the scrambled eggs onto the center of each crepe, followed by the mushrooms mixture and top with half of the feta cheese.
24. Carefully, fold each crepe like a burrito.
25. Divide the crepes onto warmed serving plates and top each with the zucchini salsa and feta evenly.
26. Enjoy with a drizzling of the tomato sauce.

CREPES
for Lovers

Prep Time: 35 mins
Total Time: 50 mins

Servings per Recipe: 6
Calories   351.9
Fat   16.5g
Cholesterol   87.1mg
Sodium   136.4mg
Carbohydrates   50.3g
Protein   5.0g

Ingredients

Crepes
2 large eggs
1/4 C. unsweetened cocoa powder
1/4 C. all-purpose flour
2 tbsp. sugar
2 tbsp. butter, melted
1/8 tsp. salt
1/4 C. milk
Pam cooking spray

Filling
4 oz. sweet chocolate
1/4 C. whipping cream
1 (21 oz.) cans cherry pie filling
Garnish
whipped topping
chocolate flavored syrup

Directions

1. For the crepes: in a bowl, add the flour, sugar, cocoa and salt and mix well. Add the milk, eggs and butter and beat until well combined and smooth.
2. Cover the bowl and refrigerate for about 30 minutes.
3. Place a lightly greased crepe pan over medium heat until heated through. Place about 1/4 C. of the mixture and tilt the pan to spread in a thin layer. Cover the pan and cook for about 1 1/2 minutes.
4. Repeat with the remaining mixture.
5. Meanwhile, for the filling: in a pan, add the cream and chocolate over low heat and cook for about 5 minutes, mixing continuously.
6. Stir in the pie filling and remove from the heat.
7. Place the warm filling onto the center of each crepe and fold like a burrito. Enjoy with a topping of the chocolate syrup.

Florida
Citrus Crepes

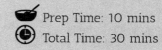

Prep Time: 10 mins
Total Time: 30 mins

Servings per Recipe: 3
Calories	405.0
Fat	8.4g
Cholesterol	141.0mg
Sodium	169.8mg
Carbohydrates	65.5g
Protein	15.2g

Ingredients

1 1/2 C. flour
1/2 tbsp. sugar
1/2 tsp. baking powder
1 1/2 C. milk
1/2 C. orange juice
2 eggs
1/2 tsp. vanilla

1 tsp. orange zest
1/2 C. orange juice
1 tsp. cornstarch

Directions

1. In a food processor, add the flour, sugar and baking powder and pulse until combined.
2. Add the eggs and pulse on low speed until well combined.
3. Slowly, add the orange zest, 1/2 C. of the orange juice, milk and vanilla and beating continuously on medium heat until smooth.
4. In a frying pan, add 1 tsp. of the oil over medium heat and cook until heated through.
5. Place about 1/4 C. of the mixture and tilt the pan to spread in a thin layer.
6. Cook until golden brown from both sides.
7. Carefully, roll the crepe and transfer onto a plate.
8. Repeat with the remaining mixture.
9. For the sauce: in a pan, add the cornstarch and remaining orange juice and beat until well combined.
10. Place the pan over heat and cook until thickened, mixing often.
11. Remove from the heat.
12. Enjoy the crepes with a topping of the sauce.

CHERRY
Cream Cheese Crepes

Prep Time: 1 min
Total Time: 2 mins

Servings per Recipe: 6
Calories   324.2
Fat   13.9g
Cholesterol   37.5mg
Sodium   144.2mg
Carbohydrates   48.2g
Protein   4.9g

Ingredients

12 prepared crepes
1 tbsp. cooking oil
Filling
8 oz. light cream cheese
8 oz. mascarpone cheese
1/3 C. Splenda sugar substitute
Cherry Sauce
20 oz. frozen pitted cherries, thawed
2/3 C. sugar

1/3 C. cranberry juice
1/3 C. water
1/4 C. lemon juice
2 tbsp. cornstarch
1/4 C. water
Garnish
12 tbsp. whipped topping, thawed

Directions

1. For the filling: in a bowl, add the mascarpone, cream cheese and splenda and beat until smooth. Place 1 heaping tbsp. of the filling mixture onto the middle of each prepared crepe.

2. Carefully, roll each crepe like a burrito. In a frying pan, add the oil over medium heat and cook until heated through. Place the crepes in batches and cook for about 3-4 minutes. Transfer the crepes onto a plate. For the sauce: in a pot, add the sugar, cherries, cranberry juice and 1/3 C. of the water over medium-high heat and cook until boiling, mixing occasionally. Meanwhile, in a bowl, add the cornstarch and 1/4 C. of the water and mix until well combined.

3. Add the cornstarch mixture into the pan of the cherry mixture and cook until boiling, mixing continuously.

4. Cook for about 1 minute, mixing continuously.

5. Remove from the heat and stir in the lemon juice.

6. Place the cherry sauce over the crepes and enjoy with a topping of the whipped topping.

Buckle
Crepes

Prep Time: 25 mins
Total Time: 25 mins

Servings per Recipe: 12
Calories	81.0
Fat	2.2g
Cholesterol	36.2mg
Sodium	133.7mg
Carbohydrates	11.3g
Protein	3.9g

Ingredients

2 C. skim milk
1/2 C. whole wheat flour
1/2 C. all-purpose flour
2 eggs
1 tbsp. honey

1 tbsp. vegetable oil
1/2 tsp. salt
1/4 tsp. butter

Directions

1. In a food processor, add all ingredients except the butter and pulse until well combined.
2. In a frying pan, add butter over medium heat and cook until melted.
3. Place about 3-4 tbsp. of the mixture and tilt the pan to spread in a thin layer.
4. Cook until golden brown from both sides.
5. Repeat with the remaining mixture.
6. Enjoy.

EUROPEAN
Currant Crepes

Prep Time: 10 mins
Total Time: 10 mins

Servings per Recipe: 1
Calories   1509.1
Fat   31.9g
Cholesterol   694.2mg
Sodium   581.9mg
Carbohydrates   263.7g
Protein   48.3g

Ingredients

1 C. all-purpose flour
1 pinch salt
3 eggs
1 3/4 C. milk
peanut oil, for pan frying
6 tbsp. dried currants

1/2 C. sugar
2 lemons, juice of

Directions

1. In a bowl, add the flour, salt, milk and eggs and with an electric mixer, beat on medium speed until well combined.
2. Grease a crepe with the oil and place over medium heat until heated through.
3. Place about 3 tbsp. of the mixture and tilt the pan to spread in a thin layer.
4. Spread about 1/2 tbsp. of the currants on top and cook until golden brown.
5. Carefully, change the side and cook until golden brown.
6. Repeat with the remaining mixture.
7. Arrange the crepes onto a platter.
8. Sprinkle each crepe with the sugar and then, drizzle with the lemon juice.
9. Carefully, roll each crepe and enjoy.

Chopped
Chicken Crepes

Prep Time: 30 mins
Total Time: 45 mins

Servings per Recipe: 4	
Calories	195.3
Fat	6.6g
Cholesterol	62.7mg
Sodium	518.6mg
Carbohydrates	26.6g
Protein	6.9g

Ingredients

Crepes
3/4 C. flour
1 C. milk
1 egg
1/2 tsp. salt
Filling
1 onion, chopped fine
1 tbsp. butter

1 C. broth
pepper
allspice
1/2 lb. leftover meat or chicken chopped
2 tbsp. flour
1 tbsp. finely chopped parsley

Directions

1. For crepes: in a bowl, add all the ingredients and beat until well combined. Keep aside for about 30 minutes.
2. Place a lightly greased frying pan over medium heat until heated through. Place about 2 tbsp. of the mixture and tilt the pan to spread in a thin layer. Cook until golden brown from both sides.
3. Repeat with the remaining mixture.
4. In a skillet, add the butter and cook until melted.
5. Add the onion and stir fry for about 4-5 minutes.
6. Add the chicken, 1/2 C. of the broth and seasonings and stir to combine. In a bowl, dissolve the flour into the remaining broth until smooth. Add the flour mixture into the chicken mixture, stirring continuously. Stir in the parsley and remove from the heat.
7. Place the chicken mixture onto each crepe evenly.
8. Carefully, roll each crepe and enjoy with a garnishing of the parsley.

CREPE
Parmigiana

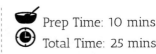 Prep Time: 10 mins

Total Time: 25 mins

Servings per Recipe: 4
Calories   383.4
Fat   19.6g
Cholesterol   56.4mg
Sodium   1106.4mg
Carbohydrates   35.1g
Protein   18.9g

Ingredients

1 lb. eggplant, peeled and cut into 8
(1/4-inch) slices
oil
8 tsp. dried basil
salt & pepper, to taste
1 (26 oz.) jars marinara sauce

6 oz. fresh Baby Spinach
1 tbsp. water
15 oz. ricotta cheese
1/2 C. Italian cheese blend, plus
8 tbsp. Italian cheese blend, divided

Directions

1. Set the broiler of your oven. Coat all eggplant slices with the oil and sprinkle with 1 tsp. of the basil, salt and pepper.
2. Cook the eggplant slices under broiler for about 5 minutes.
3. Now, set your oven to 400 degrees F.
4. In a microwave-safe bowl, add the water and spinach and microwave for about 3 minutes. Drain the spinach and rinse with very cold water. Drain very well and transfer into a bowl.
5. Place about 1/4 C. of mixture onto each eggplant slice roll like a jelly-roll style. Add 1/2 C. Italian blend cheese and ricotta cheese and mix until well combined.
6. In the bottom of a 9x13-inch baking dish, place 1 C. of the marinara sauce evenly.
7. Arrange the eggplant rolls over marinara and top wit the remaining sauce.
8. Place about 1 tbsp. of the Italian cheese over each eggplant roll.
9. Cover the baking dish and cook in the oven for about 10 minutes.
10. Uncover and cook in the oven for about 3 minutes more.

Indian
Samosa Crepes

🍲 Prep Time: 30 mins
🕐 Total Time: 1 hr

Servings per Recipe: 4
Calories	556.2
Fat	22.3g
Cholesterol	163.9mg
Sodium	681.1mg
Carbohydrates	49.1g
Protein	38.6g

Ingredients

1 lb. cooked chicken, sliced
1 large potato, diced and boiled
3/4 C. all-purpose flour
1 C. milk
1 beaten egg
salt & pepper
nonstick spray coating
1 large onion, finely sliced
2 garlic cloves, minced
1 tsp. light brown sugar

2 - 3 tsp. curry powder
1 tsp. turmeric
1 (10 3/4 oz.) cans condensed cream of mushroom soup
1/4 C. milk
cilantro
yogurt
2 tbsp. melted butter

Directions

1. For the crepes: in a food processor, add the flour, butter, egg, 1 C. of the milk, salt and pepper and pulse until well combined.
2. Place a greased frying pan over medium heat until heated through.
3. Place about 2 tbsp. of the mixture and tilt the pan to spread in a thin layer. Cook until golden brown from one side.
4. Transfer the crepe onto a plate. Repeat with the remaining mixture.
5. For filling: place a greased pot over medium heat until heated through. Add the garlic and onion and cook for about 4-5 minutes, mixing occasionally. Add the brown sugar, curry powder and turmeric and stir fry for about 1 minute.
6. Add 3 tbsp. of the milk and condensed soup and stir to combine.
7. Stir in the potato and chicken and remove from the heat.
8. In a bowl, add about 3/4 C. of the soup mixture and refrigerate, covered to chill. Arrange the cooked crepes onto a smooth surface, browned side downwards. Place the chicken mixture onto each crepe evenly and carefully, roll to secure the filling.

9. In the bottom of a greased 13x9x2-inch baking dish, arrange the rolled crepes.
10. Cover the baking dish and refrigerate for about 4-20 hours.
11. Set your oven to 350 degree F.
12. Stir the reserved soup mixture well and lace over the crepes evenly.
13. Cover the baking dish and cook in the oven for about 30 minutes.
14. Enjoy hot.

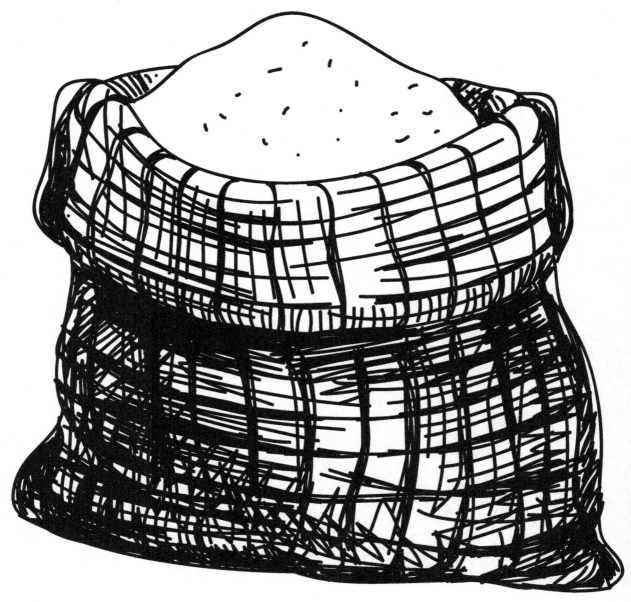

How to Make
Crepe Cake

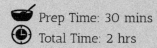 Prep Time: 30 mins
🕐 Total Time: 2 hrs

Servings per Recipe: 8
Calories   696.8
Fat   31.3g
Cholesterol   168.5mg
Sodium   505.2mg
Carbohydrates   95.1g
Protein   15.3g

Ingredients

Crepes
3 C. all-purpose flour
1 tsp. baking powder
1/4 C. sugar
1/4 C. melted butter
1/3 C. cocoa powder
3/4 tsp. salt
1/2 tsp. vanilla
4 C. milk
4 eggs
Glaze
3 oz. unsweetened baking chocolate
1/2 C. cocoa, sifted

1 1/4 C. sugar
1 C. hot water
3 tsp. espresso powder
1 dash salt
Garnish
1/2 C. butter
1/2 C. powdered sugar
cooking spray

Directions

1. For the crepe: in a food processor, add all the ingredients and pulse until well combined and smooth.
2. Transfer the mixture into a bowl and place in the fridge for about 1 hour.
3. For the glaze: in a bowl, add the espresso powder and water and mix until well combined.
4. In a pot, add the chocolate over medium-low heat and cook until melted.
5. Add the espresso mixture, cocoa powder, sugar and salt and beat until smooth.
6. Bring to a boil, stirring continuously.
7. Remove from the heat and transfer the glaze into a bowl.
8. Place in the fridge until using.
9. Place a lightly greased crepe pan over medium heat until heated through.

10. Place desired amount of the mixture and tilt the pan to spread in a thin layer.
11. Cook until golden brown from both sides.
12. Repeat with the remaining mixture.
13. Arrange 1 crepe over a plate.
14. Place glaze over the crepe evenly in a thin layer and top with another crepe.
15. Place the butter over second crepe evenly in a thin layer and top with another crepe.
16. Dust the third crepe with the powdered sugar.
17. Repeat these layers in the same way, ending with a bare crepe.
18. Place the remaining glaze over the top crepe evenly.
19. With a sharp knife, cut the stack into slices and enjoy.

Danish
Crepes

🥣 Prep Time: 15 mins
🕐 Total Time: 55 mins

Servings per Recipe: 1
Calories	109.3
Fat	4.7g
Cholesterol	45.7mg
Sodium	120.3mg
Carbohydrates	15.1g
Protein	2.0g

Ingredients

Crepe
3 eggs
3/4 C. milk
2 tbsp. granulated sugar
1/2 tsp. salt
6 - 8 tbsp. flour
Filling
2 large tart apples

1/2 tsp. cinnamon
4 tbsp. granulated sugar
1 tsp. lemon juice
1/3 C. butter
1/3 C. sugar
1/3 C. breadcrumbs

Directions

1. For the filling: in a pan, add the apples, lemon juice, sugar and cinnamon and cook until tender.
2. Remove from the heat and with a potato masher, mash the apples slightly until an applesauce like mixture is formed.
3. Keep aside to cool.
4. Set your oven to 350 degrees F before doing anything else and grease a baking dish.
5. For the crepes: in a bowl, add the flour, sugar and salt and mix well.
6. In another bowl, add the eggs and beat well.
7. Add the flour mixture and mix until well combined.
8. Add the milk and beat until well combined.
9. Place a greased crepe pan over medium heat until heated through.
10. Place desired amount of the mixture and tilt the pan to spread in a thin layer.
11. Cook until golden brown from bottom and firm on top.
12. Transfer the crepe onto a plate
13. Repeat with the remaining mixture.

14. Place the apple mixture onto the center of each crepe.

15. Carefully, roll each crepe.

16. In a bowl, add the butter, breadcrumbs and sugar and mix until a crumbly mixture forms.

17. In the bottom of the prepared baking dish, arrange the crepes and coat with the melted butter generously.

18. Top with the breadcrumb mixture evenly.

19. Cook in the oven for about 20 minutes.

20. Enjoy.

5-Star
Crepe Tiramisu

Prep Time: 15 mins
Total Time: 25 mins

Servings per Recipe: 2
Calories   173.9
Fat   8.0g
Cholesterol   80.3mg
Sodium   37.5mg
Carbohydrates   18.7g
Protein   5.2g

Ingredients

4 prepared crepes, warmed
4 ladyfingers
1 C. brewed coffee
1 fluid oz. brewed espresso
1 tsp. Splenda granular
1 tsp. pure vanilla extract
1/4 tsp. almond extract
1 C. sugar-free Cool Whip
4 tbsp. sugar-free chocolate syrup
1 tsp. unsweetened cocoa powder
4 fresh cherries, with stems, remove pits

4 tbsp. sliced almonds
Filling
8 oz. mascarpone cheese, room temp
1/4 C. sugar-free Cool Whip, thawed
2 tbsp. sugar-free chocolate syrup
1 tsp. pure vanilla extract
1/4 tsp. almond extract

Directions

1. For the filling: in a bowl, add all the ingredients and beat until well combined. Transfer the mixture into a bowl and place in the fridge for about 1 hour.
2. In a bowl, add the espresso, coffee, Splenda and both extracts and mix until well combined.
3. Place the filling mixture onto the center of each crepe evenly.
4. Coat each Lady Finger with the coffee mixture evenly to soak slightly.
5. Place 1 Lady Finger on top of the filling over each crepe.
6. Carefully, roll each crepe.
7. Arrange the crepes onto serving plates, seam side down and drizzle each with the chocolate syrup evenly.
8. Place the Cool Whip onto each crepe, followed by the almonds.
9. Garnish with fresh cherries and enjoy with a dusting of the cocoa powder.

COUNTRY
Picnic Crepes

 Prep Time: 18 mins

Total Time: 30 mins

Servings per Recipe: 4
Calories	224.1
Fat	10.6g
Cholesterol	127.1mg
Sodium	139.5mg
Carbohydrates	23.8g
Protein	7.5g

Ingredients

2 eggs, slightly beaten
1 C. whole milk
1 tsp. vanilla
1 tbsp. melted butter
1/2 C. flour, plus
2 tbsp. flour
1 1/2 tbsp. cocoa
1 1/2 tbsp. sugar

1 dash salt
1 tbsp. butter
cherry pie filling
sweetened whipped cream
chocolate syrup
chocolate shavings/curls
mint sprig

Directions

1. In a bowl, add the flour, sugar, cocoa and salt and mix well.
2. In another bowl, add the melted butter, milk, eggs and vanilla and beat until well combined. Add the flour mixture and beat until well combined and smooth. Cover the bowl and place in the fridge for about 3 hours. Remove from the fridge and stir the mixture well.
3. Lightly greased a frying pan with a little oil and place over medium-high heat until heated through.
4. Place about 1/4 C. of the mixture and tilt the pan to spread in a thin layer. Cook for about 1-2 minutes, flipping once half way through.
5. Repeat with the remaining mixture.
6. Place about 2-3 tbsp. of the cherry pie filling onto the center of each crepe.
7. Carefully, roll each crepe tightly.
8. Divide the crepes onto serving plates.
9. Top each crepe with the whipped cream, extra cherry pie filling and chocolate syrup.
10. Enjoy with a garnishing of the chocolate curls and mint sprigs.

Mushroom Asiago Crepes

Prep Time: 10 mins
Total Time: 40 mins

Servings per Recipe: 4
Calories   136.2
Fat   4.1g
Cholesterol   110.0mg
Sodium   76.7mg
Carbohydrates   18.0g
Protein   7.3g

Ingredients

Crepes
2 eggs
1/2 C. all-purpose white flour
1/2 C. milk
1 tbsp. water
1 1/2 tsp. cayenne, peppers ground
Filling
1 medium tomatoes, chopped

6 tbsp. cooking onions, chopped
8 tbsp. white mushrooms, chopped
1/4 tsp. allspice, ground
salt & pepper
4 C. spinach, fresh, chopped, firmly pressed
2 slices turkey bacon, fried, crumbled
8 tbsp. Asiago cheese, grated

Directions

1. For the crepes: in a bowl, add all the ingredients and beat until well combined.
2. Place a lightly greased frying pan over medium-high heat until heated through.
3. Place about 3 tbsp. of the mixture and tilt the pan to spread in a thin layer.
4. Cook for about 1 1/2 minutes, flipping once after 1 minute.
5. Repeat with the remaining mixture.
6. Meanwhile, for the filling: place a lightly greased skillet over medium-high heat until heated through. Add the mushroom, onion and tomato and stir fry for about 4-6 minutes.
7. Add the allspice, salt and pepper and stir to combine.
8. Add the spinach and stir fry for about 3 minutes. Stir in the bacon and remove from the heat. Set your oven to 375 degrees F.
9. Put about 2 1/2 tbsp. of the filling mixture onto 1 edge of each crepe.
10. Carefully, roll each crepe.
11. In the bottom of a baking dish, arrange the crepes and keep aside for about 10 minutes.
12. Top the crepes with the Asiago cheese and cook in the oven for about 10 minutes.
13. Enjoy warm.

BRENDA'S
Best Crepes

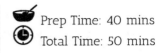
Prep Time: 40 mins
Total Time: 50 mins

Servings per Recipe: 12
Calories   261.6
Fat   8.0g
Cholesterol   75.0mg
Sodium   33.6mg
Carbohydrates   46.1g
Protein   2.3g

Ingredients

Curd
1/3 C. unsalted butter
1 (12 oz.) Apricot Preserves
4 large egg yolks, slightly beaten
1 tsp. fresh lemon juice
1/16 tsp. salt
1/2 C. frozen extra creamy whipped topping, thawed
Crepes
6 (9 inch) ready-to-use crepes

1 (28 oz.) cans sliced peaches, sliced caramel-swirl ice cream, with caramel swirl
1 (12 oz.) jars Smucker's® Orchard's Finest® Northwest Triple Berry Preserves, warmed
1/3 C. sliced almonds, toasted

Directions

1. For the curd: in a pot, place the butter over medium heat until melted. Add the egg yolks, preserves, lemon juice and salt and beat until well combined. Cook for about 7-8 minutes, mixing continuously. Remove from the heat and transfer the mixture into a bowl. Keep aside to cool. Add the whipped topping and with an electric mixer, beat on medium speed until smooth.

2. Cover the bowl and refrigerate to chill completely.

3. Place a dry frying pan over medium heat until heated through.

4. Add the almonds and cook until toasted, shaking the pan frequently. Place 1/3 C. of the curd over each crepe evenly.

5. Cut each crepe in half and carefully, fold in half.

6. Divide the crepes onto serving plates and top each with peach slices, followed by the ice cream and berry preserves.

7. Enjoy with a sprinkling of the almonds.

Hawaiian
Honey Crepes

🥣 Prep Time: 20 mins
🕐 Total Time: 40 mins

Servings per Recipe: 1
Calories	403.4
Fat	8.2g
Cholesterol	64.7mg
Sodium	233.0mg
Carbohydrates	78.8g
Protein	8.5g

Ingredients

95 g all-purpose flour, gluten-free
120 ml water
60 ml milk
1 egg
1 tbsp. coconut oil
1/4 tsp. salt
1 nonstick cooking spray
500 g mangoes, ripe, peeled, pitted and

1/2-inch cubes
1 stick cinnamon
2 tbsp. instant coffee powder, black, instant, dissolved in 2 tbsp. hot water
2 tbsp. lemon juice
3 tbsp. coconut sugar crystals
2 tbsp. honey

Directions

1. For the crepes: in a bowl, add all the ingredients and beat until well combined.
2. Place a lightly greased frying pan over medium-high heat until heated through.
3. Place about 80 ml of the mixture and tilt the pan to spread in a thin layer.
4. Cook for about 1 1/4 minutes, flipping once after 45 seconds.
5. Repeat with the remaining mixture.
6. For the filling: in a nonstick pot, add all the ingredients over low heat and cook for about 15-20 minutes.
7. Place the filling onto the center of each crepe evenly.
8. Carefully, fold each crepe and enjoy.

SAVORY
Apricot Crepes

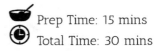 Prep Time: 15 mins

Total Time: 30 mins

Servings per Recipe: 1
Calories	1350.9
Fat	66.6g
Cholesterol	872.1mg
Sodium	1030.1mg
Carbohydrates	135.4g
Protein	49.9g

Ingredients

1 C. all-purpose flour
1 tbsp. sugar
1/4 tsp. salt
2 tsp. sugar
1 1/2 C. whole milk
4 eggs

3 tbsp. unsalted butter, melted
1 tbsp. smooth cashew butter
1 tbsp. apricot fruit spread

Directions

1. In a food processor, add all the ingredients and pulse until well combined.
2. Transfer the mixture into a bowl and place in the fridge for about 20-25 minutes.
3. Place a lightly greased frying pan over medium-high heat until heated through.
4. Place about 1/4 C. of the mixture and tilt the pan to spread in a thin layer.
5. Cook until golden brown from both sides.
6. Repeat with the remaining mixture.
7. Enjoy warm.

Roasted
Ricotta Crepes

Prep Time: 1 hr
Total Time: 1 hr

Servings per Recipe: 6	
Calories	485.1
Fat	38.5g
Cholesterol	140.1mg
Sodium	341.8mg
Carbohydrates	15.2g
Protein	22.1g

Ingredients

Crepes
3 eggs
3 C. plain flour
3 and 3/4 C. of milk
pinch of salt
butter
1 - 2 chicken breast fillet, chopped, small pieces

2 C. tomato puree
300 ml cooking cream
3 - 4 tbsp. tomato paste
750 g fresh ricotta
120 g Baby Spinach
2 tsp. vegetable Vegeta
1 C. grated cheddar cheese

Directions

1. For the crepes: in a bowl, add the flour, milk, eggs and salt and mix until well combined. Place in the fridge for about 30 minutes.
2. Lightly grease a crepe pan and place over medium heat until heated through. Place desired amount of the mixture and tilt the pan to spread in a thin layer. Cook until golden brown from both sides.
3. Repeat with the remaining mixture. Set your oven to 350 degrees F.
4. For the filling: in a lightly greased pan, add the chicken and sear until done completely. Add the cream, tomato puree and tomato paste and cook for about 2-3 minutes. Add the Vegeta and stir to combine well. With a slotted spoon, transfer the chicken pieces onto a plate, leaving the sauce in the pan.
5. In the bowl of the chicken, add the spinach and ricotta and mix well. Place the chicken mixture onto each crepe evenly.
6. Carefully, roll each crepe. In the bottom of a baking dish, arrange the crepes and top with the reserved sauce evenly, followed by the cheddar cheese. Cook in the oven until cheese begins to crisp.
7. Enjoy hot.

MASCARPONE
Fruit Crepes

 Prep Time: 15 mins
Total Time: 35 mins

Servings per Recipe: 6
Calories	180.6
Fat	8.2g
Cholesterol	1.7mg
Sodium	99.4mg
Carbohydrates	27.0g
Protein	1.3g

Ingredients

6 crepes
1/3 C. vanilla yogurt
4 oz. mascarpone cheese, softened
2 tbsp. splenda artificial sweetener
1 1/2 tsp. vanilla
1 C. blueberries
1/8 C. chopped pecans
3 medium bananas, 1/2-inch thick
slices crosswise

1/4 C. brown sugar
1/2 tsp. cinnamon
1/4 C. margarine, melted
2 tsp. lemon juice
whipped cream

Directions

1. Set your oven to 350 degrees F before doing anything else.
2. In a bowl, add the cinnamon and brown sugar and mix well.
3. In the bottom of a casserole dish, arrange the banana slices.
4. Drizzle the banana slices with the margarine and lemon juice and dust with the cinnamon sugar.
5. Cook in the oven for about 20 minutes.
6. Meanwhile, for the filling: in a bowl, add the mascarpone cheese and vanilla yogurt and beat until smooth.
7. Add the pecans, Splenda and vanilla and stir to combine well.
8. Place the yogurt mixture onto each crepe evenly and top with the blueberries.
9. Carefully, roll each crepe.
10. Remove the bananas from the oven.
11. Place the bananas mixture over the crepes evenly.
12. Enjoy with a topping of the whipped cream.

Tuscan
Crepes

Prep Time: 30 mins
Total Time: 1 hr

Servings per Recipe: 4
Calories   168.8
Fat   4.0g
Cholesterol   158.6mg
Sodium   93.0mg
Carbohydrates   24.1g
Protein   7.9g

Ingredients

3 eggs
1 C. water
1 C. flour
1 pinch salt

vegetables or olive oil

Directions

1. In a food processor, add all the ingredients except the oil and pulse until well combined.
2. Lightly grease a frying pan with the oil and place over medium-high heat until heated through.
3. Place about 1/4 C. of the mixture and tilt the pan to spread in a thin layer.
4. Cook until golden brown from both sides.
5. Repeat with the remaining mixture.
6. Enjoy warm.

SEPTEMBER
Apple Crepes

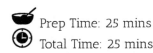

Prep Time: 25 mins
Total Time: 25 mins

Servings per Recipe: 6
Calories   559.1
Fat   22.1g
Cholesterol   131.1mg
Sodium   96.4mg
Carbohydrates   87.8g
Protein   7.8g

Ingredients

Crepes
1 C. whole milk
2 large eggs
1 C. flour
1/4 C. unsalted butter, melted
2 tbsp. icing sugar
1/4 C. unsalted butter for cooking crepe
Filling
2 tbsp. unsalted butter

6 golden delicious apples, peeled, cored and sliced
2 tsp. ground cinnamon
1/4 tsp. allspice
2/3 C. honey
1/3 C. apple cider
1 tbsp. butter
1 pint vanilla ice cream

Directions

1. For the crepes: in a food processor, add all the ingredients and pulse until well combined. Place in the fridge until using.

2. For the filling: in a skillet, add 2 tbsp. of the butter over medium-high heat and cook until melted. Add the apples and cook for about 5 minutes, stirring occasionally. With a slotted spoon, place the apples into a bowl.

3. In the same pan, add the remaining butter, apple cider, honey, cinnamon and allspice and cook until slightly thick, stirring frequently. Remove from the heat and place the honey sauce over the apples.

4. Stir the mixture well and with a foil, cover the bowl to keep warm. Place a lightly greased crepe pan over medium heat until heated through.

5. Place desired amount of the mixture and tilt the pan to spread in a thin layer. Cook until golden brown from both sides. Repeat with the remaining mixture.

6. Place the apple filling onto half of each crepe and top with the ice cream. Carefully, fold crepe over the filling and enjoy.

Oriental
Glazed Chicken Crepes

🥣 Prep Time: 25 mins
🕐 Total Time: 45 mins

Servings per Recipe: 4
Calories   447.0
Fat   17.7g
Cholesterol   196.1mg
Sodium   693.7mg
Carbohydrates   39.4g
Protein   31.4g

Ingredients

3/4 C. plain flour
salt
1 C. milk
2 eggs
2 tbsp butter
1/2 C. Hoisin sauce

2 1/2 C. cooked chicken
1 cucumber
6 green onions

Directions

1. For the crepes: in a bowl, add the eggs and milk and beat well.
2. In another bowl, sift together the flour and pinch of salt.
3. With your hands, make a well in the center of the flour mixture.
4. In the well, add the egg mixture and mix until well combined.
5. With a plastic wrap, cover the bowl and keep aside for about 15 minutes.
6. Lightly grease a frying pan with some butter and place over medium heat until heated through.
7. Place about 2 tbsp. of the mixture and tilt the pan to spread in a thin layer.
8. Cook for about 3 minutes, flipping once after 2 minutes.
9. Repeat with the remaining mixture.
10. Place the sauce over each crepe and top with the chicken, followed by the cucumber and onion.
11. Carefully, roll each crepe and enjoy.

CREPES
of Quinoa

Prep Time: 10 mins
Total Time: 30 mins

Servings per Recipe: 1	
Calories	28.4
Fat	0.8g
Cholesterol	31.0mg
Sodium	21.2mg
Carbohydrates	3.0g
Protein	1.8g

Ingredients

1/3 C. quinoa flour
1/4 C. brown rice flour
2 tsp. cornstarch
2 large eggs

2 egg whites
1 C. almond milk

Directions

1. In a bowl, add the cornstarch and flours and mix well.
2. Add the almond milk, eggs and egg whites and beat until well combined and smooth.
3. Place a lightly greased frying pan over medium-high heat until heated through.
4. Place about 2 tbsp. of the mixture and tilt the pan to spread in a thin layer.
5. Cook for about 1 1/2 minutes, flipping once after half way through.
6. Repeat with the remaining mixture.
7. Enjoy warm.

Café
Crepes

Prep Time: 5 mins
Total Time: 25 mins

Servings per Recipe: 4
Calories   239.4
Fat   10.6g
Cholesterol   116.8mg
Sodium   357.4mg
Carbohydrates   26.8g
Protein   8.4g

Ingredients

2 large eggs
1 C. milk
2 tbsp. unsalted butter, melted and cooled slightly
1 C. flour
1/2 tsp. salt
Optional Fillings
Greek yogurt

light whipped topping
seasonal berries
peanut butter
honey
banana
nutella

Directions

1. In a bowl, add the flour and salt and mix well.
2. In a bowl, add the eggs and with a wire whisk, beat well.
3. Add the milk and beat well.
4. Add the melted butter and beat well.
5. Add the flour mixture and beat until smooth.
6. Keep aside for about 30 minutes.
7. Place a nonstick frying pan over medium heat until heated through.
8. Place about 1/4 C. of the mixture and tilt the pan to spread in a thin layer.
9. Cook until golden brown from both sides.
10. Repeat with the remaining mixture.
11. Enjoy warm with the filling of your favorite condiments.

PITTSBURGH
Mushroom Crepes

Prep Time: 24 hrs
Total Time: 24 hrs 30 mins

Servings per Recipe: 4
Calories	735.6
Fat	51.1g
Cholesterol	413.0mg
Sodium	1452.7mg
Carbohydrates	39.7g
Protein	29.0g

Ingredients

Crepe Batter
2 C. milk
1 tbsp. sugar
1 tsp. salt
3 tbsp. butter, melted
1/2 C. buckwheat flour
3/4 C. flour

3 eggs
Fillings
1/2 lb. turkey bacon
1/2 C. mushroom
4 eggs
1/2 C. cheese, grated

Directions

1. For the crepes: in a bowl, add all the ingredients and beat until well combined. Place in the fridge overnight.
2. Remove from the fridge and keep aside at room temperature for about 30 minutes before cooking. Meanwhile, heat a skillet and cook the bacon for about 4-5 minutes. Add the mushrooms and cook for about 6-7 minutes. In a lightly greased frying pan, cook the eggs until scrambled. Place a lightly greased frying pan over medium-high heat until heated through.
3. Place about 1/4 C. of the mixture and tilt the pan to spread in a thin layer.
4. Cook until golden brown from both sides.
5. Transfer the crepe onto a plate.
6. Immediately, place some bacon mixture and eggs onto the crepe.
7. Carefully, roll the crepe and immediately top with a little cheese.
8. Repeat with the remaining crepe mixture, bacon mixture and cheese.
9. Enjoy.

Polynesian
Crepe Glaze

🥣 Prep Time: 10 mins
🕐 Total Time: 25 mins

Servings per Recipe: 10
Calories   330.3
Fat   0.3g
Cholesterol   0.0mg
Sodium   1.8mg
Carbohydrates   84.8g
Protein   0.8g

Ingredients

1 1/2 quarts mangoes, chunks
3 1/2 C. sugar
1 quart roasted pecan

1/4 C. water

Directions

1. In a heavy-bottomed pan, add the water, mangoes and sugar and cook until boiling.
2. Set the heat to low and cook for about 10-15 minutes, mixing frequently.
3. Stir in the nuts and remove from the heat.
4. Keep aside to cool completely.
5. Fill your crepes with the sauce and enjoy.

ALMOND
Oat Crepes

 Prep Time: 5 mins

Total Time: 6 mins

Servings per Recipe: 4
Calories	94.2
Fat	2.5g
Cholesterol	52.8mg
Sodium	17.8mg
Carbohydrates	13.0g
Protein	4.8g

Ingredients

1 egg
1/2 C. oats
1/2 C. almond milk

Directions

1. In a food processor, add the oats and pulse until ground finely.
2. In a bowl, add the oat flour, almond milk and egg and beat until well combined.
3. Place a lightly greased crepe pan over medium heat until heated through.
4. Place desired amount of the mixture and tilt the pan to spread in a thin layer.
5. Cook until golden brown from both sides.
6. Repeat with the remaining mixture.
7. Enjoy warm.

Spicy
Mexican Corn Crepes

Prep Time: 10 mins
Total Time: 1 hr 10 mins

Servings per Recipe: 10
Calories   152.6
Fat   4.6g
Cholesterol   85.0mg
Sodium   298.5mg
Carbohydrates   21.8g
Protein   5.8g

Ingredients

2 Serrano chilies, stemmed and seeded
2 sprigs fresh cilantro or 2 sprigs parsley
4 eggs
1 C. water
1 C. skim milk
1 tsp. salt
1/2 tsp. baking powder

1 C. cornmeal
1 C. flour, all-purpose
1 tbsp. sugar
1 1/2 tbsp. safflower oil

Directions

1. In a food processor, add the cilantro and chilies and pulse until minced.
2. Add the remaining ingredients and pulse until smooth.
3. Transfer the mixture into a bowl and keep aside at room temperature for about 45-60 minutes.
4. Place a lightly greased frying pan over medium-high heat until heated through.
5. Place about 1/4 C. of the mixture and tilt the pan to spread in a thin layer.
6. Cook until golden brown from both sides.
7. Repeat with the remaining mixture.
8. Enjoy warm.

MANHATTAN
Apple Crepes

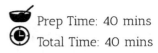 Prep Time: 40 mins
Total Time: 40 mins

Servings per Recipe: 4
Calories   469.8
Fat   19.4g
Cholesterol   235.3mg
Sodium   230.9mg
Carbohydrates   63.4g
Protein   12.4g

Ingredients

Batter
4 eggs
1 tbsp. corn oil
1 C. milk
1 C. all-purpose flour
1 pinch salt
Filling
1 (16 oz.) cans apple pie filling

1 McIntosh apple, peeled, cored, diced
1/2 lemon, juice of
1/4 C. chopped pecans
1/2 tsp. cinnamon
2 - 4 tbsp. butter

Directions

1. In a bowl, add the oil and eggs and beat until frothy and light.
2. Add the milk and beat until well combined.
3. Add the flour and salt and beat until well combined.
4. Cover the bowl and place in the fridge for about 20 minutes.
5. Place a lightly greased frying pan over medium-high heat until heated through. Place about 1/4 C. of the mixture and tilt the pan to spread in a thin layer. Cook until golden brown from both sides.
6. Repeat with the remaining mixture.
7. For the filling: in a bowl, add the apple, pecans, pie filling, lemon juice and cinnamon and mix well.
8. Place 1 tbsp. of the filling onto the center of each crepe.
9. Carefully, fold the crepe over the filling.
10. In a skillet, add 2 the butter and cook until melted.
11. Add the crepes in batches and cook until golden brown from both sides. Enjoy hot.

Gorgonzola
Cheddar Chicken Crepes

🥣 Prep Time: 1 hr
🕐 Total Time: 1 hr 20 mins

Servings per Recipe: 6	
Calories	681.5
Fat	48.0g
Cholesterol	375.0mg
Sodium	1350.5mg
Carbohydrates	27.9g
Protein	36.0g

Ingredients

1 C. flour
1 1/2 C. milk
3 eggs
4 egg yolks
1 tbsp. vegetable oil
1 tsp. vegetable oil
cooking spray
2 tsp. salt
pepper
1 tbsp. minced garlic
1/2 tsp. onion powder

12 oz. Baby Spinach
12 oz. broccoli
16 oz. chicken breasts, cooked and cubed
1/2 C. gorgonzola, crumbled
1 C. sharp cheddar cheese, shredded
2/3 C. cream
1 lemon, juice of
1/2 C. butter

Directions

1. Set your oven to 350 degrees F before doing anything else.
2. For the filling: in a wok, add 1 tbsp. of the oil and cook until heated.
3. Add the broccoli and garlic and cook for about 3-4 minutes.
4. Stir in the spinach, onion powder, salt and pepper and stir fry for about 2-3 minutes.
5. In a bowl, add the chicken, cooked broccoli mixture, Gorgonzola, 1/4 C. of the cheddar and mix well.
6. Add 1 egg and mix until well combined.
7. For the crepes: in a bowl, add the flour, 2 eggs, milk, 1 tsp of the vegetable oil and 1/4 tsp. of the salt and beat until well combined.
8. Lightly greased frying pan with the cooking spray and place over medium heat until heated through.
9. Place about 1/4 C. of the mixture and tilt the pan to spread in a thin layer.
10. Cook until golden brown from both sides.

11. Repeat with the remaining mixture.

12. Place the chicken mixture onto the center of each crepe evenly.

13. Carefully, roll each crepe.

14. In the bottom of a 13x9x2-inch baking dish, arrange the crepes and top with the remaining cheddar cheese.

15. Cook in the oven for about 20 minutes.

16. Meanwhile, for the Hollandaise sauce: in a pan, add 2/3 C. of the cream, 4 egg yolks, juice of 1 lemon and 1 tsp. of the salt over low heat and cook until mixture becomes thick, mixing continuously.

17. Remove from the heat and add the butter, stirring continuously until melted.

18. Enjoy the crepes with a topping of the Hollandaise sauce.

South Indian
Chicken Rice Crepes

Prep Time: 30 mins
Total Time: 1 hr

Servings per Recipe: 5
Calories	647.3
Fat	13.7g
Cholesterol	31.7mg
Sodium	67.9mg
Carbohydrates	100.1g
Protein	30.4g

Ingredients

Crepe
2 C. long-grain rice
1 C. black lentils
1 C. mung beans
2 tbsp. ginger, chopped
2 green chilies, chopped
salt
1 C. water
2 tbsp. oil
clarified butter
Filling
1/2 lb. minced chicken

1 C. finely dices red bell pepper
1 C. finely diced celery
1 C. finely chopped scallion
1 tsp. garlic, minced
1 tsp. ginger, minced
2 fresh green chilies, minced
1/2 C. fresh tomato, finely chopped
salt and pepper
2 tbsp. cooking oil

Directions

1. For the crepes: in a large bowl of the water, soak the lentils and rice overnight.
2. Drain the soaked rice mixture well and rinse completely.
3. In a food processor, add the rice mixture, ginger, chilies and water and pulse until a smooth paste is formed.
4. Transfer the mixture into a bowl and stir in the salt.
5. Place in the fridge for about 7 hours.
6. Lightly grease a crepe pan with the clarified butter and place over medium-low heat until heated through.
7. Place desired amount of the mixture and tilt the pan to spread in a thin layer.
8. Cook until golden brown from both sides.
9. Repeat with the remaining mixture.
10. For the filling: in a nonstick skillet, add the oil and coo until heated.

11. Add the ginger and garlic and stir fry for about 45 seconds.

12. Stir in the chicken, salt and pepper and cook for about 5-6 minutes.

13. Add the bell pepper, tomatoes, celery, scallion and chilies and stir to combine.

14. Set the heat to low and cook for about 5-6 minutes.

15. Stir in the salt and pepper and remove from the heat.

16. Keep aside to cool.

17. Coat each cooked crepe with a thin layer of the clarified butter.

18. Place about 1 1/2 tbsp. of the filling mixture in the center of each crepe.

19. Carefully, fold each crepe and enjoy.

How to Make
a Crepe

Prep Time: 10 mins
Total Time: 20 mins

Servings per Recipe: 4
Calories	51.2
Fat	0.3g
Cholesterol	0.3mg
Sodium	135.0mg
Carbohydrates	2.6g
Protein	9.2g

Ingredients

6 egg whites
1/8 C. dry rolled oats, cooked
1/8 C. nonfat cottage cheese

15 g protein powder

Directions

1. In a bowl, add all the ingredients and beat until well combined.
2. Place a lightly greased crepe pan over medium-low heat until heated through.
3. Place desired amount of the mixture and tilt the pan to spread in a thin layer.
4. Cook until golden brown from both sides.
5. Repeat with the remaining mixture.
6. Enjoy warm.

GREEK STYLE
Crepes

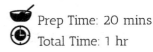

Prep Time: 20 mins
Total Time: 1 hr

Servings per Recipe: 4
Calories	334.1
Fat	13.1g
Cholesterol	168.8mg
Sodium	418.3mg
Carbohydrates	36.9g
Protein	19.0g

Ingredients

2 - 3 bunches spinach, washed and stalks removed
1 onion, chopped
feta cheese, crumbled
1/2 C. grated Romano cheese
1 carton ricotta cheese, small carton
1/2 tsp. ground allspice
salt
freshly ground black pepper
1 egg, lightly beaten
Crepes
125 g all-purpose flour

1 pinch salt
2 eggs
1 1/4 C. milk
3 tsp. butter, melted
oil
Garnish
tomato sauce
mozzarella cheese

Directions

1. Set your oven to 350 degrees F before doing anything else and lightly, grease a baking dish.
2. For the filling: in a microwave-safe bowl, add the spinach in batches and microwave, covered until slightly wilted.
3. Drain well and with your hands, squeeze the liquid completely.
4. Then, chop the spinach roughly.
5. In a bowl, add the spinach, onion, Romano, ricotta and feta and blend well.
6. Add the egg, allspice, salt and pepper and mix until well combined.
7. In a bowl, add the flour and salt and mix well.
8. Now, sift the flour mixture into another bowl.
9. Add some milk and eggs and beat until well combined.
10. Add the remaining milk and beat until well combined.

11. Add the melted butter and beat until well combined.
12. Lightly grease a frying pan with a little oil and place over high heat until heated through.
13. Place about 3-4 tbsp. of the mixture and tilt the pan to spread in a thin layer.
14. Cook for about 1 1/2 minutes, flipping once after 1 minute.
15. Repeat with the remaining mixture.
16. Place the spinach mixture onto the center of each crepe evenly.
17. Carefully, fold each crepe into a parcel shape.
18. In the bottom of the prepared baking dish, arrange the crepes and top with the tomato sauce, followed by the mozzarella cheese.
19. Cook in the oven for about 15-20 minutes.
20. Enjoy hot.

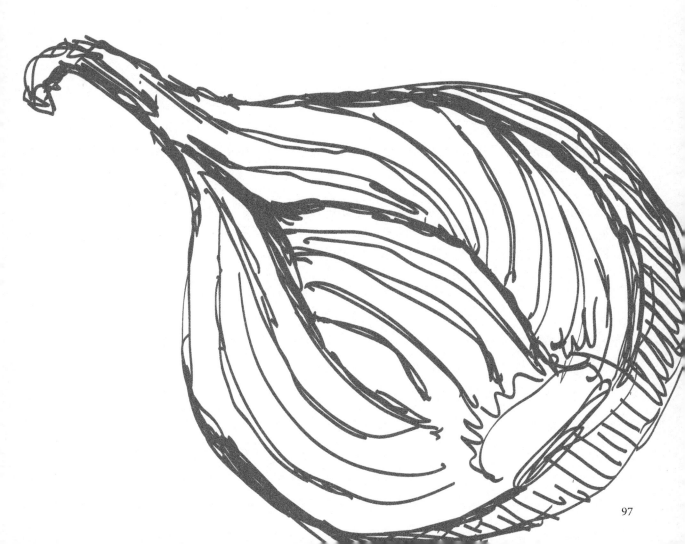

AUSTRALIAN
Hazelnut Crepes

Prep Time: 5 mins
Total Time: 45 mins

Servings per Recipe: 4
Calories   335.8
Fat   15.8g
Cholesterol   114.2mg
Sodium   119.2mg
Carbohydrates   38.0g
Protein   8.7g

Ingredients

1/2 C. all-purpose flour
2 large eggs
1 pinch salt
1 C. milk
1 tsp. orange extract

cooking spray
8 tbsp. nutella
powdered sugar

Directions

1. In a bowl, add the flour, salt, eggs, milk and orange extract and beat until well combined.
2. Lightly grease a crepe pan with the cooking spray and place over medium-high heat until heated through.
3. Place about 1/4 C. of the mixture and tilt the pan to spread in a thin layer.
4. Cook for about 5 minutes, flipping once after 3 minutes.
5. Repeat with the remaining mixture.
6. Place about 1 tbsp. of nutella onto each crepe evenly.
7. Carefully, roll each crepe and enjoy with a dusting of the powder sugar.

Full Dinner
Crepes (Broccoli and Chicken)

🥣 Prep Time: 20 mins
🕐 Total Time: 50 mins

Servings per Recipe: 6	
Calories	515.5
Fat	42.4g
Cholesterol	119.5mg
Sodium	784.6mg
Carbohydrates	15.1g
Protein	21.1g

Ingredients

1/4 C. butter
1/4 C. all-purpose flour
2 C. chicken broth
2 tsp. Worcestershire sauce
3 C. cheddar cheese, grated
2 C. sour cream

1 1/2 lb. broccoli, cooked & drained
2 C. chicken, cooked & chopped
12 crepes

Directions

1. Set your oven to 350 degrees F before doing anything else.
2. in a pot, add the butter over medium heat and cook until melted.
3. Stir in the flour and cook until thick and bubbly, mixing continuously. Stir in the Worcestershire sauce and chicken broth and cook until thick, mixing continuously.
4. Remove from the heat and stir in 2 C. of the cheddar cheese until melted completely. In a bowl, place the sour cream.
5. Slowly, add the hot cheese sauce, mixing continuously until well combined. Put the chicken and broccoli onto each crepe evenly and top each with 1 tbsp. of the cheese sauce.
6. Carefully, fold each crepe over the filling.
7. In the bottom of a baking dish, arrange the crepes and top with the remaining cheese sauce evenly, followed by the remaining cheddar cheese. Cover the baking dish and cook in the oven for about 20-30 minutes. Enjoy hot.

CREPES
with Nuts and Spinach

Prep Time: 25 mins
Total Time: 1 hr 45 mins

Servings per Recipe: 4
Calories   602.7
Fat   41.9 g
Cholesterol   166.6mg
Sodium   241.5mg
Carbohydrates   32.9 g
Protein   29.2 g

Ingredients

2/3 C. whole wheat flour
1 egg
2/3 C. plain yogurt
3 tbsp. water
1 tbsp. olive oil
1 package frozen spinach, thawed and pureed
1 pinch of ground allspice
salt and pepper
fresh cilantro (to garnish)
Filling
1 tbsp. olive oil

3 scallions, thinly sliced
1 C. ricotta cheese
4 tbsp. plain yogurt
3/4 C. grated Gruyere cheese
1 egg, lightly beaten
1 C. unsalted cashews
2 tbsp. chopped parsley
1 pinch cayenne pepper

Directions

1. Set your oven to 350 degrees F before doing anything else and grease a shallow baking dish.
2. For the crepe: in a bowl, add the oil, yogurt, egg and water and beat until well combined.
3. In another bowl, add the flour and salt and mix well.
4. Now, sift the flour mixture into a second bowl.
5. Slowly, add the egg mixture, whisking continuously until well combined.
6. Add the spinach, allspice and pepper and stir to combine.
7. For the filling: in a skillet, add the oil and cook until heated through.
8. Add the scallions and stir fry for about 2-3 minutes.
9. With a slotted spoon, transfer the scallion onto a paper towel lined plate to drain.
10. In a bowl, add the yogurt, ricotta and half of the Gruyere and beat until well combined.
11. Add the egg, parsley, salt and cayenne and beat until well combined.

Crepes with Nuts and Spinach

12. Place a lightly greased frying pan over medium-high heat until heated through.
13. Place about 3-4 tbsp. of the mixture and tilt the pan to spread in a thin layer.
14. Cook for about 5 minutes, flipping once after 3 minutes.
15. Repeat with the remaining mixture.
16. Place some of the filling onto the center of each crepe evenly.
17. Carefully, fold each crepe in envelope style.
18. In the bottom f the prepared baking dish, arrange the crepes and top with the remaining filling, followed by the remaining cheese.
19. Cook in the oven for about 15 minutes.
20. Enjoy hot with a garnishing of the cilantro sprigs and lemon wedges.

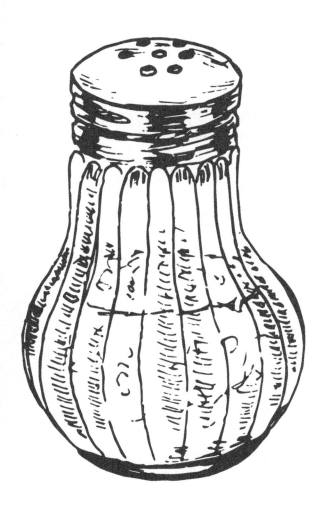
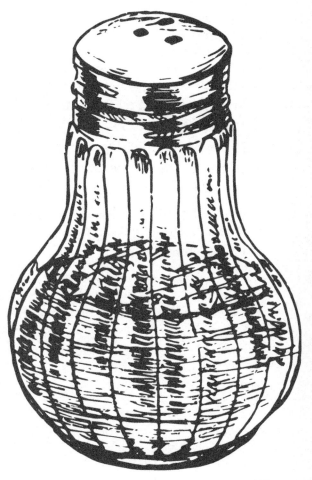

MORNING FROST
Crepes

Prep Time: 5 mins
Total Time: 20 mins

Servings per Recipe: 4
Calories   241.5
Fat   11.0g
Cholesterol   226.7mg
Sodium   153.8mg
Carbohydrates   24.8g
Protein   9.8g

Ingredients

1 C. all-purpose flour
1 C. water, plus
2 tbsp. water
4 large eggs
2 tbsp. melted butter

1 pinch salt
1/3 C. chopped of fresh mint

Directions

1. In a blender, add all the ingredients except the mint and pulse until well combined.
2. Transfer the mixture into a bowl and place in the fridge for about 1 hour.
3. Remove from the fridge and stir in the mint.
4. Place a lightly greased crepe pan over medium heat until heated through.
5. Place desired amount of the mixture and tilt the pan to spread in a thin layer.
6. Cook for about 2 minutes, flipping once after 1 1/2 minutes.
7. Repeat with the remaining mixture.
8. Enjoy warm.

New England
Crepes

Prep Time: 40 mins
Total Time: 50 mins

Servings per Recipe: 4
Calories   285.7
Fat   19.0g
Cholesterol   139.6mg
Sodium   402.4mg
Carbohydrates   5.2g
Protein   23.9g

Ingredients

8 crepes
1/4 tsp. black pepper
1 lb. freshly shucked lobster meat
1 tsp. fresh squeezed lemon juice
1/4 C. clarified butter
1 C. cooked well drained spinach
1/4 C. minced onion
1/4 C. white sauce

1/2 C. sliced mushroom
1 C. hollandaise sauce, optional
1 tsp. chopped garlic
1/4 C. chopped parsley
1/4 C. chopped walnuts

Directions

1. Set your oven to 350 degrees F before doing anything else.
2. In a skillet, add the oil over medium heat and cook until heated through.
3. Add mushroom, onions and garlic and stir fry for about 5-6 minutes.
4. Stir in the white sauce, spinach, walnuts, lemon juice and black pepper and remove from the heat.
5. Place about 2 oz. of the lobster onto each crepe, followed by the spinach mixture.
6. Carefully,, roll each crepe.
7. In the bottom of a baking dish, arrange the crepes, folded side down.
8. Cook in the oven for about 10 minutes.
9. Divide the crepes onto serving plates and top each with the Hollandaise sauce, followed by the parsley.
10. Enjoy with a sprinkling of the paprika.

CHESTNUT
Crepes
(No Gluten)

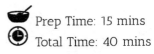

Prep Time: 15 mins
Total Time: 40 mins

Servings per Recipe: 4

Calories	268.8
Fat	23.4g
Cholesterol	212.0mg
Sodium	158.1mg
Carbohydrates	7.0g
Protein	7.3g

Ingredients

1 1/2 C. chestnut flour, sifted
1/8 tsp. salt
1 tbsp. sugar
1 1/4 C. whole milk
1 tsp. vanilla extract

3 large eggs
6 tbsp. unsalted butter, melted

Directions

1. In a bowl, add the flour, sugar and salt and mix well.
2. In another bowl, add the milk, eggs and vanilla and beat until well combined.
3. Add the flour mixture and beat until well combined.
4. Add 2 tbsp. of the butter and mix until well combined.
5. Grease a crepe pan with a little butter and place over medium heat until heated through.
6. Place about 1/4 C. of the mixture and tilt the pan to spread in a thin layer.
7. Cook until golden brown from both sides.
8. Repeat with the remaining mixture.
9. Enjoy warm.

3-Cheese
Dinner Crepes

Prep Time: 1 hr
Total Time: 1 hr 30 mins

Servings per Recipe: 4
Calories	767.0
Fat	44.1g
Cholesterol	294.0mg
Sodium	1542.7mg
Carbohydrates	44.4g
Protein	46.7g

Ingredients

Crepes
1 C. water
1 C. flour
2 eggs
1/8 tsp salt
vegetable oil
Filling
1 lb. ricotta cheese
1 C. grated mozzarella cheese, packed

1/2 C. grated Parmesan cheese
1 tsp fresh garlic
1 egg
2 tbsp fresh finely chopped parsley
salt and black pepper
2 C. favorite pasta sauce
2 C. grated mozzarella cheese

Directions

1. Set your oven to 350 degrees F before doing anything else and grease a 9x9-inch baking dish. For the crepes: in a bowl, add the eggs, flour, salt and 1 C. of the water and beat until well combined.
2. Grease a frying pan with a little oil and place over medium heat until heated through. Place about 2-3 tbsp. of the mixture and tilt the pan to spread in a thin layer.
3. Cook for about 4 minutes, flipping once after 1 minute. Repeat with the remaining mixture.
4. For the filling: in a bowl, add the egg, Parmesan, 1 C. of the mozzarella, parsley, garlic, salt and pepper and beat until well combined. Place 3 tbsp. of the filling onto the center of each crepe.
5. Carefully, fold the crepe over the filling.
6. In the bottom of the prepared baking dish, place about 1 C. of the pasta sauce evenly.
7. Place the rolled crepes over the pasta sauce, seam side down and top with the remaining pasta sauce, followed by the mozzarella cheese. Cook in the oven for about 25-30 minutes. Enjoy hot.

PICNIC
Crepes

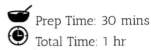

Prep Time: 30 mins
Total Time: 1 hr

Servings per Recipe: 6
Calories   196.2
Fat   0.6g
Cholesterol   0.7mg
Sodium   66.5mg
Carbohydrates   42.0g
Protein   6.6g

Ingredients

Crepe
1 1/4 C. all-purpose flour
1 pinch salt
2 egg whites
7/8 C. skim milk
2/3 C. orange juice
oil, for frying
yogurt or light crème fraiche, to serve

Filling
4 medium oranges
2 C. blueberries

Directions

1. Set your oven to 400 degrees F before doing anything else.
2. For the crepes: in a bowl, sift together the salt and flour.
3. With your hands, make a well in the center of the flour mixture.
4. In the well, add the milk, egg whites and orange juice and with a whisk, beat until a smooth and bubbly mixture is formed.
5. Place a lightly greased crepe pan over medium heat until heated through.
6. Place desired amount of the mixture and tilt the pan to spread in a thin layer.
7. Cook until golden brown from both sides.
8. Repeat with the remaining mixture.
9. In the bottom of a baking sheet, arrange 6 small oven proof bowls, upside down.
10. Arrange 1 crepe over each bowl to form the baskets.
11. Cook in the oven for about 10 minutes.
12. Remove from the oven and carefully, lift the baskets from the bowls.
13. Meanwhile, pare a thin orange rind slice from one orange and cut into strips finely.
14. In a pan of the boiling water, add the orange strips and cook for about 30 seconds.

15. Drain the orange strips in a colander well and rinse under cold running water.
16. Keep aside to drain.
17. Remove the peel and white pith from all the oranges.
18. Divide each orange into segments, reserving the dripping juice into a bowl.
19. In a microwave-safe bowl, add the blueberries and orange segments alongside the juice and microwave until just warmed.
20. Divide the fruit mixture into each crepe basket evenly.
21. Enjoy with a topping of the rind strips.

WEST INDIAN
Cheese Crepes

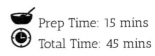

Prep Time: 15 mins
Total Time: 45 mins

Servings per Recipe: 4
Calories	223.0
Fat	3.0g
Cholesterol	47.4mg
Sodium	48.4mg
Carbohydrates	42.5g
Protein	6.7g

Ingredients

125 ml light coconut milk
2 tbsp. brown sugar
1/2 tsp. vanilla essence
2 bananas
200 g low-fat ricotta
1 tbsp. coconut
Crepes
80 g plain flour

185 ml skim milk
1 egg
1/2 tsp. vanilla essence
cooking spray

Directions

1. For the crepes: in a bowl, add the egg, milk and vanilla essence and beat until well combined. In another bowl, place the flour.
2. Add the egg mixture and beat until blended nicely.
3. Place a lightly greased crepe pan over medium heat until heated through. Place about 2 tbsp. of the mixture and tilt the pan to spread in a thin layer. Cook for about 3 minutes, flipping once after 2 minutes. Repeat with the remaining mixture.
4. In a pan, add the sugar, coconut milk and vanilla essence over low heat and cook until sugar dissolves, mixing continuously.
5. Set the heat to high and cook until boiling.
6. Now, set the heat to medium and cook for about 2-3 minutes.
7. Add the banana and cook for about 1 minute, tossing frequently.
8. Place the ricotta over each crepe evenly.
9. Carefully, fold each crepe over ricotta.
10. Place the crepes onto serving plates and top each with the banana mixture.
11. Enjoy with a garnishing of the coconut.

Flavors
of November
Crepes

Prep Time: 10 mins
Total Time: 30 mins

Servings per Recipe: 16
Calories   76.0
Fat   3.1g
Cholesterol   26.1mg
Sodium   19.9mg
Carbohydrates   9.6g
Protein   2.2g

Ingredients

1 C. all-purpose flour
1 1/3 C. milk
2 eggs
2 tbsp. brown sugar
2 tbsp. cooking oil
1 tbsp. light molasses

1/2 tsp. ground cinnamon
1/4 tsp. ground ginger
1/4 tsp. ground allspice

Directions

1. In a bowl, add all the ingredients and with an electric mixer, beat until well combined.
2. Place a lightly greased frying pan over medium heat until heated through.
3. Place about 2 tbsp. of the mixture and tilt the pan to spread in a thin layer.
4. Cook until golden brown from both sides.
5. Repeat with the remaining mixture.
6. Enjoy.

HOLIDAY
Leftover Crepes

 Prep Time: 50 mins

Total Time: 1 hr 20 mins

Servings per Recipe: 6
Calories	438.0
Fat	20.0g
Cholesterol	148.1mg
Sodium	1101.1mg
Carbohydrates	55.0g
Protein	10.0g

Ingredients

2/3 C. all-purpose flour
2/3 C. whole milk
6 tbsp. warm water
2 large eggs
2 large egg yolks
1/4 C. chopped fresh chives
4 tbsp. unsalted butter, melted

1/2 tsp. salt
2 1/4 C. shredded roast turkey
2 1/4 C. leftover prepared stuffing
1 1/4 C. cranberry sauce
2 C. turkey gravy

Directions

1. In a food processor, add the flour, milk, eggs, egg yolks, butter, water, chives and salt and pulse until blended nicely.
2. Transfer the mixture into a bowl and keep aside for about 30 minutes. Set your oven to 375 degrees F and arrange a rack in the center of the oven. Grease a frying pan with a little butter and place over medium-high heat until heated through.
3. Place about 2-3 tbsp. of the mixture and tilt the pan to spread in a thin layer. Grease a 15x0x2-inch baking dish with the butter.
4. Grease a frying pan with a little butter and place over medium-high heat until heated through. Place about 3 tbsp. of the mixture and tilt the pan to spread in a thin layer. Cook for about 1 3/4 minutes, flipping once after 1 minute. Repeat with the remaining mixture.
5. Place about 3 tbsp. of the turkey onto the center of each crepe, followed by 3 tbsp. of the stuffing and 1 tbsp. of the cranberry sauce.
6. Carefully, roll each crepe to secure the filling.
7. In the bottom of the prepared baking dish, place the crepes, seam side down and top with 1 1/2 C of the gravy evenly.
8. Cook in the oven for about 20 minutes.
9. Enjoy hot alongside the remaining cranberry sauce and gravy.

Harvest
Crepes

🥣 Prep Time: 45 mins
🕐 Total Time: 55 mins

Servings per Recipe: 8
Calories	215.7
Fat	13.0g
Cholesterol	82.0mg
Sodium	221.5mg
Carbohydrates	17.6g
Protein	7.6g

Ingredients

2 large eggs
1 C. milk
1/3 C. water
1 C. all-purpose flour, preferably bleached
1/4 tsp. salt
2 tbsp. butter, melted

butter, for coating the pan
3/4 C. Brie cheese, thinly sliced
2 small apples, thinly sliced
1 tbsp. butter, melted
1/4 C. walnuts, chopped

Directions

1. In a food processor, add the flour, 2 tbsp. of the melted butter, water, milk, eggs and salt and pulse until well combined.
2. Transfer the mixture into a bowl and place in the fridge for about 2 hours. Grease a frying pan with a little butter and place over medium-high heat until heated through.
3. Place about 2-3 tbsp. of the mixture and tilt the pan to spread in a thin layer.
4. Cook for about 1 1/2 minutes, flipping once after 1 minute.
5. Repeat with the remaining mixture.
6. Set your oven to 375 degrees F.
7. Place 1 cheese slices over each crepe, followed by 3 apple slices.
8. Carefully, fold each crepe.
9. In the bottom of a 12x18-inch baking dish, arrange the crepes.
10. Coat the crepes with the remaining melted butter and top with the walnuts.
11. Cook in the oven for about 8-10 minutes.
12. Enjoy hot.

ITALIAN
Herbed Crepes

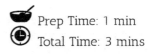 Prep Time: 1 min

Total Time: 3 mins

Servings per Recipe: 1

Calories	42.0
Fat	2.0g
Cholesterol	30.3mg
Sodium	57.0mg
Carbohydrates	4.2g
Protein	1.6g

Ingredients

1/2 C. all-purpose flour
2 tbsp. all-purpose flour
2 eggs
1/2 C. milk
1/2 C. cold water, plus
2 tbsp. cold water
1 1/2 tbsp. melted butter

1/4 tsp. salt
Spice Mix (use 1/4 C.)
1 tsp. dried tarragon
1 tbsp. fresh chives, snipped
1 tbsp. fresh parsley, finely chopped
1 tbsp. dried chervil

Directions

1. In a food processor, add all the ingredients except the herbs and pulse until well combined.
2. Transfer the mixture into a bowl and stir in the herbs.
3. Place in the fridge for about 1 hour.
4. Place a lightly greased frying pan over medium-high heat until heated through.
5. Place about 2-3 tbsp. of the mixture and tilt the pan to spread in a thin layer.
6. Cook until golden brown from both sides.
7. Repeat with the remaining mixture.
8. Enjoy.

Georgia
Crepe Cake

Prep Time: 15 mins
Total Time: 25 mins

Servings per Recipe: 6
Calories	531.4
Fat	23.6g
Cholesterol	127.6mg
Sodium	440.6mg
Carbohydrates	71.9g
Protein	9.1g

Ingredients

Filling
1 (8 oz.) packages cream cheese, softened
1 C. powdered sugar
1 tsp. almond extract
1/2 C. seedless raspberry jam
1 (15 1/4 oz.) cans peach slices in heavy syrup, drained
1 (7 oz.) cans whipped cream

Batter
2 eggs
1 C. milk
2 tbsp. vegetable oil
1 C. buttermilk pancake mix
nonstick cooking spray

Directions

1. In a food processor, add the oil, milk and eggs and pulse until well combined. Add the pancake mix and pulse until smooth.
2. Place a lightly greased frying pan over medium-high heat until heated through.
3. Place about 1/4 C. of the mixture and tilt the pan to spread in a thin layer. Cook until golden brown from both sides.
4. Repeat with the remaining mixture.
5. Meanwhile, in a bowl, add the powdered sugar, cream cheese and almond extract and with a hand mixer, beat until smooth.
6. Arrange a crepe onto a plate.
7. Place about 2 tbsp. of the cream cheese mixture over the crepe evenly.
8. Repeat with the remaining 6 crepes and cream cheese mixture.
9. Place the last bare crepe on top.
10. Top with the peach slices in a decorative pattern.
11. With a sharp knife, cut into 8 wedges.
12. Enjoy with a topping of the whipped cream.

CENTRAL
European Style Crepes

 Prep Time: 10 mins

Total Time: 20 mins

Servings per Recipe: 3

Calories	324.6
Fat	14.2g
Cholesterol	155.7mg
Sodium	737.0mg
Carbohydrates	37.2g
Protein	11.2g

Ingredients

2 eggs
1 tsp. sugar
3/4 tsp. salt
1 C. white flour
1 C. milk

2 tbsp. butter, melted
butter

Directions

1. In a bowl, add the eggs, salt and sugar and beat until well combined.
2. Add the flour, melted butter and milk and with a whisk, beat until smooth.
3. In a crepe pan, add a little water and place over medium-low heat and cook until melted.
4. Place desired amount of the mixture and tilt the pan to spread in a thin layer.
5. Cook until golden brown from both sides.
6. Repeat with the remaining mixture.
7. Enjoy.